networking
know-how!

networking
know-how!
connecting for success

ZOE CUNNINGHAM

urbanepublications.com

First published in Great Britain in 2016 by Urbane Publications Ltd
Suite 3, Brown Europe House, 33/34 Gleamingwood Drive, Chatham, Kent ME5 8RZ
Copyright © Zoe Cunningham, 2016

The moral right of Zoe Cunningham to be identified as the author of this work has
been asserted in accordance with the Copyright, Designs and Patents
Act of 1988.

A CIP catalogue record for this book is available from the British Library.

ISBN 9781911129066
EPUB 9781911129073
KINDLE 9781911129080

Design and Typeset by Julie Martin
Cover by Julie Martin
Printed and bound by CPI Group (UK) Ltd, Croydon, CR0 4YY

urbanepublications.com

I'd like to dedicate Networking Know-How to to my husband Sean Williams, who has always believed in me and taught me how to believe in myself. I'd also like to thank Justine Solomons, who took me to my first networking event and encouraged me to get started with networking. And Ghilaine Chan, my co-founder at Exponential, who's helped me to refine my networking technique and meet even more great people.

contents

contents

introduction

After completing a mathematics degree, I started my career working as a software developer. For five years I talked to machines, in their language, or to my colleagues who were also coders. I socialised with people I knew; I was terrified when I had to sit at a table without my husband at a friend's wedding because my husband was the Best Man and was sitting on the top table.

I hadn't heard of networking, and if I had I would have been appalled by it. I had a general antipathy to all forms of selling and I would have understood networking to be cold calling but in person – truly horrifying!

Gradually as my career developed my role expanded and I took on responsibility for talking to clients, eventually heading up the support team. Now I talked to clients on a regular basis, but in a support rather than a sales role. I considered the two to be opposites. Working in support I was helping people, whereas in sales they were trying to get things from people. I knew that sales was what paid my salary, but I considered it a kind of necessary evil rather than a genuinely useful function.

My first experience with the sales function of the

company came in the form of "technical sales" – I was lured in by the fact that it was a role for technical people. My responsibility was for scoping and estimating the work that needed doing. I was assured that all sales was left to the salesperson proper, who accompanied me.

As I worked more closely with the sales team, a lot of my fears diminished. Sometimes the work could be high pressure and nerve wracking, but the emotional rewards of winning a contract more than made up for this. Further, the "real" sales work that the sales team, rather than the technical team, did seemed to not be work at all. A lot of it was lunches, coffees or just general meetings with clients, and everyone seemed to be having a lot of fun. I decided that maybe I would give it a go.

This move to the sales team turned out to be one of the smartest of my career. Everything I had previously thought about sales was incorrect. I learned a new phrase "consultative selling", which described how to sell complex software systems. You can only do this in partnership with the client. You are on their side, not on the opposing team. What's more, learning how to solve other people's problems using the skills and services that you have available (which is how I would now describe the sales process) is applicable to almost every scenario where you want to achieve a specific outcome. Which, it turns out, is almost always.

True to my expectations, the first few networking events that I attended were horrifying. I remember following around my manager and mentor Justine Solomons (now founder of the successful digital publishing network Byte the Book) like a lost puppy, terrified of going to meet new people. At one event for BBC suppliers, the first person that Justine and I met was a similarly network-phobic supplier. I remember really clearly Justine giving me and the other supplier a pep talk as we were clinging to her coat-tails. "You need to go and meet people. Off you go. Shoo!"

Hundreds of events later, I have learnt from the hard master of experience how easy networking can be if you approach it with the right attitude. I've learnt how to "fake it until you make it" and how to make meaningful connections by being authentically myself. Most of all I've found not only that I can have fun at networking events, but also that having fun makes me more successful.

If I could go back in time and tell myself this ten years ago, I wouldn't have believed it.

So that's my personal journey from shrinking violet to life and soul of the party. But unless you have been through this journey yourself, you might be thinking "Why bother? Yes, I can see how perhaps I too could come to love networking, but I don't see that I need to."

Networking is often seen as a tool for salespeople and recruiters, for the professionals that rely on a "little black book" of contacts in order to get the job done. If you work on the front line or as a manager, you might be forgiven for thinking that it's of no use to you, however much fun you might (possibly!) be able to have.

My journey to understanding why networking is for everyone, not just salespeople, started with a fundamental shift in how I viewed the world. For everyone, our training for the real world starts in a schooling system, almost all of which operate in a way that is, it turns out, not at all like the real world.

When you are working to get ahead in school, you are operating in a win-lose environment. If you help your friend to study and get an A grade, it doesn't help your marks. Worse, most grading systems are relative, so by helping your friend to get an A you are actually reducing your chances to get one.

Lots of people operate with a win-lose mindset. If your colleague wins the promotion, you don't. If everyone in your organisation becomes more talented, you become less valuable. If a similar company to yours makes a sale, your market share diminishes.

It is natural to think this way. In the formative years of the human race, resources were scarce. Human beings were very often in the situation that if someone else ate, you did not. You had to be prepared to fight to stay alive. There are also situations today that are win-lose. If you are competing against others, for example in a professional sport, only one person can take home the gold medal.

However, nowadays the win-lose situations are mostly artificially constructed. School, sports and political elections are systems that we have created to function in this way. Remarkably, once you start to think in the opposite way to win-lose, which is win-win, you will start to see that win-win applies to almost everything in your life.

For example, what if… your colleague winning a promotion means that you now have a useful friend in a more senior position who can help you with your agenda? What if… everyone in your organisation becoming more talented means that collectively you achieve more, win more clients and gain an improved professional reputation? What if… your competitor makes a sale, does a great job and as a result increases the total market available for everyone?

Win-win is the concept that I can get what I want *by helping you to get what you want*. Win-win is a common negotiation strategy for ongoing relationships. Rather than beating down a supplier to a price that is uneconomical you instead want to negotiate a deal that works for you and for them, so that they want to continue working with you longer term.

Also, when you deal with other people with a win-win rather than a win-lose attitude you are much more likely to get to a solution. If you are working together you can trust each other and pool information and contacts, making you both at least twice as likely to make progress towards your goals. (In reality it will often be more than twice as likely as information does not combine in a linear fashion – for example two pieces of information put together may uncover a third.)

You may still be sceptical. "Surely", you will say, "sometimes people are your competitors and that's the end of it?" I truly believe that if you can learn to start to look at the world through the lens of win-win, you will find that situation happens much less often that you would think. Even when two people are applying for the same job, they often do so with very different aims – one may want to switch departments and position themselves for a more senior role, while another may be looking for a management challenge and a payrise. If you are lucky you may work for a company where you could suggest a different split of the role to get you both what you want. But even if not, suppose that you get the role? You will always need good people around you, so having thought about what your competitor wants, you may be able to use your new position to find a role for them that benefits you both.

One of the reasons that win-win is so powerful in today's world is that we are all completely interconnected. There is very little that you can want from life that you won't need someone else's help to achieve. Every modern job relies on a series of intertwined organisations in order to make it possible. Take my previous role as a coder. That role wouldn't have existed without the sales team to close business, or indeed without the clients to demand it. It also would have been a lot more painful and less fun without payroll software, administrative and support staff and our office chef.

Networking as a tool allows you to reach the people who can help you best. It allows you to make contact with powerful individuals who you would otherwise have not had access to. Most of all it allows you to uncover serendipitous opportunities that you could not have planned for, for the simple reason that you were not aware that they existed.

In this book I cover in detail the why, who and how of networking. I go even further into the benefits of networking and give some examples of amazing opportunities that could only have arisen that way.

I explain why you fear networking, by drawing out the examples of bad networking behaviour that I know you will have been subjected to on previous experiences, and which you will have mistaken as being what networking is. This chapter also provides a handy guide for what not to do when networking!

Understanding who you are is central to being a successful networker. I show you how to find your strengths and key personality traits, and how to then pare them down to a succinct core that can quickly communicate to other people what you are about. You might well find that you are more interesting than you realised!

Confidence can play a large part in successful networking and I include a section of hints and tips to get you started. This sections shows how to get out there and networking, and how to use your successes to increase your confidence further, leading you into a virtuous circle.

While you do not have a very developed network, the easiest way to begin to expand it is by meeting people at events, whether these are purposely designed for networking, or just a place where lots of people are gathered. This can be the most difficult and nerve wracking way of networking so I prepare you for how to shine in that environment.

Much more pleasant is to network over a coffee or glass of wine with an engaging and influential person. I share the secrets of how to find and then approach these people, plus how to manage any tête-á-têtes for best results.

Online networking is a whole new ball game, with different rules and conventions. You will need different skills to make an impact here, but a few simple tips will help you to support your in person networking with an online strategy.

All of this is building up to the one great secret of networking, which I reveal at the end of the book. This one fact is well known by all super-networkers, and can completely transform how successful your are, as well as how much you enjoy networking. I finish by giving you some suggested next steps to cement you learning and a bibliography of great networking books for further reading.

I've come a long way since my initial days of panic standing in a room full of strangers, and I've really enjoyed writing it all down in a book to help others to follow the same journey a little more quickly and less painfully!

In fact, I now love networking so much that I started my own company, Exponential, to help people working in tech startups expand and grow their businesses by making fortuitous connections. In just under two years we've helped over eight hundred people working not just in startups but also in corporates, the media and in startup related services. Following the principle of win-win, we achieve twice as much as any other organisation, as in order to help one person, we must also be helping the person we have matched them with. For every startup who has been featured in the media, we have also given a journalist an exclusive story. For every startup who has received free law advice, we have also created a potential client and future source of revenue for a law firm. For every co-founder, we have found another co-founder, and for every new client for a new app, website or service, we have solved a problem for that user that no-one else could solve.

I hope that by following the principles in this book you too can come to feel the joy in making connections between people that I do and I wish you the best of luck in applying it to your own personal dreams and goals.

Zoe Cunningham
Founder, Exponential

why network?

"Acquaintances, in sort, represent a source of social power, and the more acquaintances you have the more powerful you are."

Malcolm Gladwell, *The Tipping Point*

If you work in a profession where you need to close business – as a salesperson, recruitment agent or lawyer, for example – you are probably reading this book thinking that you already know why you network. It's to find a client, or meet someone who might one day introduce you to a client. You will have a good idea of why you network, who you network with and what the benefits are.

If you're networking in this way, that's great and you're definitely a step up from someone who doesn't network at all, but you're only getting a fraction of the benefits that you could be getting. For some reason, it seems very clear to us that we need to meet new people in order to get business, but we often don't realise all the

other, less direct, benefits that we could be achieving if
we changed our networking style slightly.

These indirect benefits are the reason that you should
be networking even if you're not in a profession in
which it is usual to network. In business today, we are
used to working in a calculated, rational way. We make
plans, set goals and break down our strategic vision
into concrete step by step paths that will take us to
our ultimate objectives. This is great and I am all for
planning, but networking is not something that works
like this.

Something that we are coming to have a better
understanding of is the idea of a complex system. Since
the work of the great Mandelbrot in the 1960s, the areas
of chaos theory and complexity have come to be more
widely studied. My favourite recent book on the subject
is Antifragile by the banker Nassim Taleb. Complexity
theory best explains my understanding of the effects
of networking. By making more and more connections
and sending out your actions through these channels,
there will be associated reactions. You can better shape
the results of networking by choosing which of these to
act on, than by aiming for a specific outcome since, like
the butterfly flapping its wings, you cannot control the
outcome.

I'm aware that I sound a little bit like a mystic, and I

assure you that I'm not one, so I'll try to explain with a different metaphor. Imagine that for every action you take there is a tiny probability that someone will respond with a positive action that would be of use to you. The more people that you are connected to, in both your direct and indirect networks (by an indirect network I mean the people who know the people who know you, even though you don't know them directly) the higher the probability of such an action.

To take a simple example, imagine that you are in need of a graphic designer, at a good price because the work that you need done is not yet revenue generating. If you have a small network (and you are not a designer yourself), you will need to get lucky – perhaps someone's sister is just starting out, or perhaps a friend has recently used a designer that he can recommend. But if you have a network of hundreds or thousands of people, the numbers are large enough that you don't need to be lucky – someone you know will be able to help you.

It's not what you know, it's who you know

When I give talks on networking I often start with the phrase "It's not what you know, it's who you know".

I enjoy using this phrase to explain networking both because it is a simple piece of folk wisdom, but also because many people have a very negative emotional reaction to it. I was brought up to think very negatively of nepotism and of people finding jobs for their friends. The "Old Boys' Network" an informal network of men who were at school or college together is a great example of this. Very rarely is this brought up as a great way for people to quickly and easily find great people who can do the job. Instead it is considered a bastion of elitism – a way of keeping the best jobs for the rich (and male) elite.

I have a lot of sympathy for this position. I am a great believer in diversity and in social mobility. I think that both of these make the world a better place and companies and institutions stronger. However resisting the two related concepts that people are more likely to do something for a friend than for a stranger, and that no-one can recommend you if they haven't heard of you (no matter how good your work is), is as futile as denying the existence of gravity. It will still drag you downwards.

Another correlated bugbear that I have only managed to overcome by really understanding networking is the fact that my parents were not super well connected people with loads of contacts. Perhaps if my dad had been pop star Steven Tyler, I too could have got a starring role in Lord of the Rings, or if my mum had been a national agony aunt I could have become a famous food critic. This again misses the point. We are all born to unequal playing fields, or to use the bridge analogy, with a different set of cards. What matters is how you play the hand that you are dealt.

So once you realise that the secret to success is knowing the right people, you can either feel trapped in the world knowing that you were not born to the right contacts, or you have another choice. You can get out and start meeting people.

Meet the game changers

For the purposes of your business or personal goals, not all people are created equal. The most straight forward and obvious benefit of networking is that you can get to meet the people who can be useful to you. You may bump into them at an event, you may go to hear them speak and catch them afterwards or you may be introduced by a mutual connection.

If you are not used to networking then very often it can feel like an imposition for you to take up someone's time just in case they can be helpful to you. Now that I understand about the principle of win-win, it is clear to me that when networking is done best, this is not the case. If you are talking to someone who could give you a job, you are sourcing a potential candidate for them, if you are talking to someone to try to make a sale, you are providing a potential solution for them and if you are asking someone to make an introduction to their friend you may well be giving them a useful gift that their friend will appreciate. Of course, the fact that good networking is win-win does not change a situation where someone is not interested in what you have to offer, and any attempts by you to rephrase it as such will add fuel to the fire. If what you have to offer is not of use after all, politely excuse yourself and move on.

Through networking I have been able to meet all kinds of people who I would have considered out of my reach. I have met the heads of television production companies, the vice-chairman of Ogilvy and Mather, TV presenter Maggie Philbin (a childhood hero) and musician Willie Dowling (my husband's childhood hero!). Everyone you consider to be "too important" to talk to you is a person just like you with a family, a career and an agenda of their own. If their agenda matches with yours, you might be able to help each other.

Another type of contact that you might make through networking, is what I call the "super-connector". Malcolm Gladwell, in his well-received book *The Tipping*

Point, referred to three factors that influenced whether a trend would take off. The first of these factors was a description of the types of people who would need to endorse the trend, and of these the "connectors" were the most important. Connectors are the people in a community who know large numbers of people and who are in the habit of making introductions. They usually know people across an array of social, cultural, professional, and economic circles, and make a habit of introducing people who work or live in different circles.

As I have become a more proficient networker and met more and more people, I have started to come into contact with these super-connectors. Last year I met a lady called Carole Stone, who is referred to on Wikipedia as "London's networking queen" and who was awarded in 2011 the title of "Best-Connected Woman in British Business" by the Institute of Directors. Her contacts are almost all themselves super-connectors and most super-connectors that I meet seem to know each other.

As Malcom says, "There are exceptional people out there who are capable of starting epidemics. All you have to do is find them."

Internal networking

I feel that I am lucky to have worked my whole life in

small organisations. Within a 100 person company there is no need for networking – everyone knows everyone else. But if you work for a large corporate it brings both confusion and overhead, and also vast opportunity. The skills that you can use in networking externally with sales contacts or potential recruits, can also be used internally to all kinds of ends.

As with most things, I suspect the most common reason that people network internally within organisations is the straightforward one. If you are connected to more people, you are more likely to hear about jobs that are available; if you have more friends in different departments, you are more likely to be recommended for a job; and if you greet everyone on an interview panel by name because you know them already, you are more likely to get the position. In short, most people network to get promoted.

That's a very valid benefit, but it's not the only one, and good connectors will be making contact for all kinds of reasons. If you know more people in more departments, you will be able to call in a favour when a task that you need is overrunning. By knowing the people who you are relying on you are likely to avoid a lot of the friction that can occur when two groups of people with different aims have to work together. You may need at some point to effect a change across the whole organisation

– imagine how much easier it would be if you had some guys on the inside in other departments!

Internal networking can be a much more accessible form of networking as you already have one thing in common with anyone you meet – you are part of the same organisation. There will likely be established ways to meet people too – if you are thinking like a networker, international conferences can becomes opportunities, rather than annoyances.

There are also likely to be many clubs that you can become part of. Some will be work related or even set up to facilitate networking. These are a great opportunity to meet others who are keen on networking but can get too work focussed. They may also attract the "bad networkers" (see the next chapter).

If you are female, there will very likely be a network to support women in leadership roles, and if there isn't one already I would suggest seizing the chance to establish one. I have found female networking groups to be very supportive, and they offer unparalleled access to senior women. You will also be able to give something back by supporting junior women, who may be unsure of their position and who could one day grow into powerful friends.

There are also social clubs, and these can be the best

places of all to network. At a common interest group you will meet people who are genuinely passionate and excited about the same things as you.

You also have the opportunity to ask for help. Everyone who is currently high up in the company will remember the people who gave them a helping hand and when time and other commitments allow, they will be keen to pay it back. It is likely (although not guaranteed) that they have also become proficient networkers and will not be surprised at all for you to ask to meet for a coffee.

Extra-curricular opportunities

We've covered the business benefits of networking quite a lot. It's true that few people without a business or career agenda are as active at networking. But networking can help with anything that you want to achieve in life that needs more than one person to achieve it, which because of the complex interconnected world that we live in, is almost everything.

Something that I come across a lot is pro-active parents who start networking on behalf of their children. I have been asked for internships and work placements, or sometimes just to have a chat about universities and planning for life. Once you are a networker, setting your children up to benefit from your contacts is automatic. If you are not, it might not have occurred to you. Think about it. Getting your child a key work placement through a contact could be more life changing for them than any amount of hard work at school.

As human beings we also (unless we work too hard) have a variety of interests and hobbies. Just like with business, most of these involve other people. You can't play badminton on your own, and even if you have a regular partner, imagine how much more enjoyable it could be if you joined a team or a league. Especially when you are new to a town, meeting people and letting them know what you have an interest in can be the best way to find these opportunities.

I have what I describe as a portfolio career, so the different between what is work and what is a hobby can be a bit blurred. I have two great example of opportunities that arose through networking. The first was that through meeting a live music and gig organiser, I found out that he also worked as a DJ on local station Shoreditch Radio, and through him I found out that there were spaces for more DJs. I've now been with Shoreditch Radio for nearly two years and it's been my longest radio job yet.

I belong to a brilliant mailing list called Women in

Technology (an example of a great online networking tool), and found all kinds of interesting opportunities through that list. I was going through an expansive phase in my career, so I answered an advert for guest bloggers for www.girlgeekchic.com. Blogging has turned into both a great hobby and a great way to meet more people.

Serendipity – opportunities you couldn't plan for

My career has been a great exercise for me in learning how to strategise and plan. The school system (certainly in the UK) maps out a path for you – do well at school, go to university, get a job – so I was used to bumbling along without thinking too much where I wanted to get to. As I learned more and more in the workplace though, it became apparent that there were many, many opportunities and many different roads to travel, and that you wouldn't get very far down any of them if you didn't stop and make a map.

I love thinking ahead and planning and for most people this is the first step towards realising their dreams. Think about what is possible (anything!), and put yourself in the best possible place to get there. On the other hand, being too single minded can mean that you miss the random chances that can throw up big opportunities. If you talk to lots of people who have made it, they attribute their success to "being in the right place at the right time". Planning to be waiting in the right place for when the right time comes along is a perfectly valid strategy, and better than leaving it to chance, but you need to ensure that you don't end up in the right place at the right time but looking in the wrong direction.

Not only are there many paths to the same end, but sometimes a chance occurrence can make us realise that we could achieve a different end, or enjoy a different experience that might be worthwhile in itself.

There is a limit to the number of things that we can plan for, and I think that many opportunities are difficult and painful to achieve via planning. Instead meeting a wide variety of people and being alert to possibilities can bring better results.

I have a large number of meetings with all kinds of different people. Some are clients, or employees, and agendas for these meetings are usually pretty straightforward. Some are with potential clients or potential networking contacts, and again I usually have an idea what to expect and what I could hope to achieve from a meeting. But every so often I accept a meeting with a person, usually someone who has been recommended to me by someone I know, and I find I have been too busy to prepare and end up attending the meeting without any idea why I am there.

Several times this has thrown my planning brain into a panic. "Time is a scarce resource," it says. "You have a zillion other things you should be doing. Why are you here?" But I have learnt something very surprising from these meetings. I have learnt that the less I plan for and prepare for a meeting, the more unusual and unexpectedly great the outcome. I am aware that this sounds like an anti-rationalist statement, but there are several reasons why I might feel like this. The first is that by having such low expectations of a meeting, any positive outcome feels like a big win. This is perfectly possible! Another explanation, however, is that by not trammelling the meeting down my pre-prepared lines I am leaving it open for serendipitous creation between myself and my guest.

I am not sure that I would advocate a completely unplanned life (as lived by the man in the wonderful novel "The 100 year old man who climbed out of a window"), but perhaps, just occasionally, it is worth meeting with people and just seeing what you have in common and how you can help each other.

Last year I had the most amazing experience as a result of one such meeting. In November I received a call from the UK Department for Trade and Industry. "Would Miss

Cunningham", inquired a very polite lady on the other end of the phone, "like to accompany the Prime Minister David Cameron on a trade delegation to China?" Well, yes she would, thank you very much.

I had just joined a tech advisory board called Labour Digital and had some other contacts in government through my work to help small software companies win more government business, so I was keen to see which of my activities had resulted in this opportunity. I immediately asked where UKTI had got my name. The lady on the phone was very apologetic. The list had been prepared by "Number 10" she explained and so I must be on a list with them.

I was very flattered at the thought of people on such a list, maybe pinned to Dave's fridge, but really this just pushed the problem back a step for me. How did I get onto that list?

I had another opportunity to find out on the trip itself. The staff from the Prime Minister's Office ("Number 10") were very supportive and came round to offer all delegates any help that they could use. I happened to join a conversation where one lady was explaining how hard it had been to get the right types of businesses for the trip. "Brilliant!" I interjected, "You are the person who will be able to answer my question of why I was selected for the trip." The lady looked slightly puzzled and then replied, "Oh no, you weren't on my list. You were recommended by UKTI."

I found it immensely entertaining that no-one would own up to inviting me on the trip. I felt a bit like a gate-crasher at a party. I was also perplexed because I was pretty sure that I didn't know anyone who worked at UKTI, and hadn't even met anyone. On further thinking, I had an idea. About a year previously I had had a speaker at one of my events who had very kindly introduced me to her mentor, who was a wonderful lady who I was bound to get on with. I had gone along and had a very enjoyable meeting, and Judith the mentor had introduced me to several useful contacts and I hadn't really thought of it again. But now I was wracking my brain for a link to UKTI, I remembered that Judith had been part of a scheme for mentoring successful startups through the UKTI. She didn't work for them in the traditional sense, but maybe she was the link that I was looking for.

It was a lovely opportunity to reconnect and find out how things were with her and it turned out that yes, indeed, she had been asked for recommendations and had mentioned my name. What an amazing chain of events.

So why not try some networking? You might end up in places you had never imagined.

Don't just network when you need something

Like people making wills when they are sick, most of us who do try networking do it when we find that we need someone. If we are looking for a new role, we are much more likely to start reaching out to people to see whether they know anyone who has something going. This is the time when we call up old friends and go for a drink or offer to stop by an old colleague's workplace for a coffee.

We do this because it works. If we don't get out there and ask people, our opportunities are much more limited. But it's not the best way to network.

We've all been there. A friend we haven't spoken to for ages phones up. Perhaps initially you are pleased to hear from them, but that feeling quickly fades when you realise that they have only phoned up because they would like you to do a favour for them. They want something from you. Or maybe even as soon as you see who's calling you get that sinking feeling that you are going to be asked to do something.

Networking works best when it's built on great human relationships. I don't want to be in contact with the type of people who only call me up when they want something. I want to be linked with people who are fun, who share my interests and who get in touch because they've thought of something that they can do for me. For those people I always go the extra mile when they do ask for a favour, and I also pro-actively think of ways to help them, so they don't even need to ask.

You might think that now's not the right time for you to network, because you're happy in your job and you don't need anything. On the contrary if you don't need anything immediately now is the very best time to start making connections. That means that the relationships will be ready when you do need something, and asking for help won't feel like an imposition. And if you network with the right people, you might even find you never get to the point where you need to call in a favour as you start getting head hunted for the exciting roles you didn't know you wanted.

Fun

We live in a culture today where people work harder than they have ever worked before. Chances are that you are reading this book at the weekend, having done a full week of long days, because you want to get ahead and you are prepared to work harder in order to do so.

If so, I admire your work ethic! Working hard is a

great skill, and is behind every single success story, especially the ones where someone seems to have been "catapulted" to fame. Working every minute of every day, however, is a trap that you need to be careful to avoid.

Lots of my friends, particularly those who work in the city have very little time for anything outside of their main job. They are expected to work late into the evening, and come in at the weekend if they are needed. While I admire hard work, dedicating all your time to one organisation, particularly a corporation, is not a great way to go.

It took me ten years of work to understand what having a good work-life balance means. I had always interpreted it to mean that you shouldn't work too hard and so an example of good work-life balance would be coming home at 5pm every day and watching TV. I am now amazed at how wrong I got that.

Work-life balance is all about where you dedicate your energy and from where you draw you sense of identity and self-esteem. If you don't have interests outside of work, then you don't have a good work life balance, no matter how short you keep your hours. Whereas if you have a great family life, an interested in science fiction and belong to a local choir, you are balancing your work identity with your identity as a parent, a sci-fan fan and a chorister.

If you are already a hard worker and you decide to take on networking as a work activity, you are not balancing out your life. In fact you are quite likely adding to the stress and pressure of your lifestyle. (I hope you don't take this the wrong way, but it will also make you quite a boring person to talk to, as we explore later in the book!) This is not good networking!

Instead networking is a great chance to find something that will make a great addition to your life and diversify your interests. Some of the best places to network are social clubs and interest groups. If you are enjoying yourself and having fun, without feeling the pressure of work, your personality will shine through and you will find it easier to make genuine connections with people.

It is a common and pernicious myth that if you are having fun you must somehow be working less hard or less diligently. In networking it is very clear that the absolute opposite is true. People want to hang out with people who are engaging, interesting and having fun. Put yourself in the places where you are that person.

the wrong lessons you learned from the bad networkers

(or *Why you hate networking*)

Time and time again I hear impassioned attacks on networking from people who have tried it, often several times, and had a very unpleasant experience. The picture I paint of networking feels totally alien to them, and they simply do not believe my description of great networkers as generous, kind-hearted and giving people.

If you too feel like this, there is a very simple reason. You have been networking with **bad networkers**. If someone spoke to you for two minutes before rushing away when someone they considered more important came along, they were a bad networker. If a slick and pushy man grabbed your hand in a firm handshake, looked you in the eye, left you with his business card and stormed off before you could catch your breath, he was a bad networker. If a power suited lady spoke at length about her very, very boring accountancy services, without letting you get a word in, she was a bad networker.

Get the idea?

In this section I outline the bad habits of networking, the malignant and persistent traits that unnecessarily terrify so many networking newbies. In debunking these attitudes, I hope I can help to reverse a terrible misfortune that has befallen networking. As human beings we learn what to do by watching how others behave. Chances are that the people you see selling to, boring or disrespecting you were themselves once horrified by this behaviour, but steeled themselves to learn it, reasoning that they needed to do so to get ahead. Networking is so powerful a tool that even if you do it as badly as these people, you will still increase your personal and business opportunities. Imagine what you could achieve if you could network and remain human! (Which is of course exactly what I will teach you in this book.)

Another handy way to use this chapter is as a list of

things to avoid doing, and ways to identify the people at events with whom you should avoid speaking.

Over-selling

I grew up with an impression of sales people as slick, pushy, disingenuous people who would sacrifice their own grandmother in order to make a sale. Since I joined the business development team and changed my role I have had countless revelations about how great, relationship-based sales people need to be exactly the opposite of this stereotype.

So I feel I bit guilty referring to this behaviour as sales, because it's behaviour that good salespeople don't engage in, even when they are selling!

If you are a salesperson, you have two ways to sell. The traditional "Del boy" method of stretching the truth to the point of lying and conning someone into buying your service who didn't want or need it, and the modern sales approach of meeting and chatting to people until you find the individuals who can make or save money by using your service. The great revelation of 20th century sales is that the latter method is much more effective. As a salesperson time is your most limited and precious resource, and you can best spend that time finding the people you can help rather than trying to convince someone to buy something that they don't want.

When I refer to overselling in a networking context I am talking about one simple behaviour. People who talk about themselves and their services without asking you any questions to find out whether the information that they are giving you is appropriate for your situation. You will be able to spot these people really easily because they will be talking, not listening, boring the person at whom they are talking and, most sadly of all, looking slightly bored themselves because they are reeling off a sales pitch rather than having an enjoyable and engaging conversation. By behaving in a self-interested way, aiming to seek out benefits for themselves, they will be breaking all of the rules in this section, alienating the people they talk to, and as a result making fewer meaningful connections.

Don't let that person be you!

Talking rather than listening

It's very tempting, especially if you are nervous, to launch into long explanations of what you do or attempt to tell amusing stories in order that there isn't a gap in the conversation. At many an event I have had the conversation lull and been panicked into thinking "What can I say? How can I be interesting?"

If you have been engaged as a speaker or other entertainer then you need to have a great message and many amusing stories. But if you are networking you only need to entertain the person that you are talking with. The best way to do that is to have a meaningful conversation, and the best way to have a meaningful conversation is to focus on listening rather than on talking.

One great to way to learn techniques to use for networking (or indeed any skill in life) is to look at people that you admire and who seem to be able to use these skills effortlessly, and to break down what they are doing. Notice what tricks they are using (even if these are probably acted out subconsciously). If you do this you will learn that all great networkers are great listeners.

They do this by following one simple rule. On meeting someone for the first time, they will ask a question about that person, rather than instantly talking about themselves. I urge you to try watching for this next time you are networking. It is quite remarkable how people do this and instantly create a great atmosphere and rapport.

One thing to note is that you need to evince genuine interest. One message that you will hear time and time again from this book is that is not possible to fake being a nice person. You can fake being a good networker (and more on that later) but whenever you interact with a person you need to be genuine. If you ask people all about their lives and don't bother to listen to the answers, this will have a counterproductive effect. The person that you are talking to will feel that you are trying to trick them into something, or that you are not a very authentic person. Or they may not think anything specific but just have a vague sense of unease and dislike.

The reason that the technique of asking questions and listening works is simple. By asking the other person to set the agenda you are much more likely to hit on a topic that really catches their interest (to look at the opposite extreme, your accountancy software is very unlikely to do this). The simple fact is that everyone enjoys to talk about themselves, especially those people who are not often asked.

I recently saw a post on LinkedIn offering another point of view on this idea. He called it "one simple technique that will make you an amazing networker". He told a story of how when he was at an event, feeling lonely and too scared to talk to anyone, a charming, witty, friendly guy came over, shook his hand confidently and started a conversation. He instantly felt at home and asked the networker what his secret was. How did he manage to be so confident? How did he manage to approach others without feeling nervous or awkward? The reply was simple. "I'm not confident," said the networker, "but I just adopt this technique when I am at events. Tell me, did you feel nervous and uncomfortable when I came over to talk to you? No. My technique is that I look for someone who looks lost and uncomfortable like me and then I go over and introduce myself and try to put them at ease."

Being boring

Listening is also a brilliant technique, because it is very hard to be actively boring when you are listening closely and taking an interest in the other person.

I cannot begin to count the number of times that someone has actively bored me at a networking event or even in a one on one meeting. It's possible that I am overly critical having worked hard on my abilities in this area and having an understanding of sales theory, but I have been extremely disappointed to be bored in the following ways.

You might have noticed that I often mention accountancy software as an example of how you might bore someone. This is based on an actual example where a whole event seemed to be centred around someone talking about accountancy software features.

No jokes, no human interest, just a detailed breakdown of software functionality. Yes, you would have been bored too.

I have been bored whenever someone talks to me non-stop without a chance for me to even interject. I cannot think of a single such monologue where I was glued to their every work, only ones where I was painfully desperate to get away.

The way that you say something also affects how boring it is. I have been on a few science communication courses that teach budding science presenters how to let their natural enthusiasm for the subject shine out. Lots of people think that at a "work" event, or for a "serious" topic you should adopt a formal and expressionless style. Also, when you are nervous and unsure of yourself your fear reaction will clamp down on your body's expressiveness. So remember to joke and laugh, and smile to get your point across. If talking about anything, talk about something that you truly love, not something that you think you should love.

The technique of asking intelligent questions (as described in the last section) isn't always the answer either. Remember that your objective is to be authentic and make a real meaningful connection with the person. I have never had as many offers of undirected help, as after I give a talk on networking to say that's "what you should do". Needless to say, when surround by a group of people who appear to be following a rulebook I grasp with joy at anyone who is just interested in an honest human conversation. (Please, please don't interpret this to mean that I am opposed to learning and to using rules while you learn. Quite the opposite. It's just worth remembering that you learn to use rules so that you can throw them away and use your instinct once you have developed it.)

I have also been bored by people using my time in a one to one meeting asking "intelligent questions" when I am actually quite busy and keen to get off. It is an uncomfortable feeling when you are happy to help but have a feeling that someone is asking questions that they are not interested in the answers to, in order to make you feel at ease! If you suspect that someone might be busy, make sure you always ask how long they have and if you come to suspect that they are "not quite there", wrap up quickly and try again another day.

I don't mean for this to be a list of horror stories about how you might actually be less interesting that you think you are. We are only human and can try to do our best. I am certain that despite all my research into and practice of networking I frequently bore people, particularly those who are different to me (sorry! if that was you). Just remember that the key is to engage the other person, and that they are much likely to remember you and your message if they have made a real connection and are engaged with what you have to say.

Being bored

"Happy people sell", trumpets The Call Centre, an all-too-real glimpse into the lives of callers in a Swansea call centre, currently into its third series on BBC. It's a cliché, but it's a cliché for a reason.

As in sales, doubly so in networking. You cannot make meaningful relationships that you can build on in the future while you are stuck in a corner wishing you were somewhere else. Recall the people who delighted you when you met them. The people who you respected and, just a tiny bit, envied. I'll bet that these people were full of energy and passion and pursuing their dreams with delight. I suspect that you cannot even recall the miserable, misanthropic networkers who were only interested in grumbling.

Relationships between human beings are incredibly complex. We are hard wired to pick up on emotional signals from other people, even when we are not consciously aware of it. Research has shown that people can reliably tell the difference between a genuine and a faked smile. You might think that you can go to a boring networking event, have a rubbish time and still make connections. Unfortunately this is not true. People will see through you.

If you are bored, chances are that you will also be boring. If you find yourself in this position, you have only one way out (apart from leaving, which is a very valid option). You need to find something that genuinely engages you. What do you most enjoy talking about? What have you previously had successful conversations over? If you have a varied number of interests, it's very likely that at least one of them will overlap with someone else at the event. Find out what the people you meet are interested in, and pounce when you uncover something that you would like to chat about. I've used this technique many a time when I was feeling tired and antisocial, and turned an event from a chore into a delight.

There is a compelling reason not to network at places that bore you. Life is short, and you only get to live it once. Don't spend your precious minutes in a flat, sterile environment that encourages the wrong type of people making relationships in the wrong kind of way. Live a little. Join a samba class, or a pottery class or a sports club and see who you can meet there.

Being disrespectful

One of the things that most saddens me is when people have been so burned by bad networkers that they start to believe that they must give up basic human decency in order to take part. I find this misconception particularly upsetting because it leads to so much unnecessary pain, both for those people who hurt themselves while they perpetuate it and for the new networkers who continue the cycle by learning the wrong thing all over again.

Once you have got your feet with networking, and started to meet the uber-networkers who go out of their way to help others, you too will be shocked by what a misapprehension it is to think that being polite and courteous is anything other than an asset.

People who consider themselves good (but "tough") businesspeople and networkers are disrespectful in a surprising number of ways. I've seen the following, and I'm sure that there are plenty more examples that you have seen too.

- People who give you their card before taking the time to find out whether you would like it.

- People who don't make eye contact because they are too busy scanning the room to see who else is there.

- People who stop mid-sentence and leave when they see the chance to talk to someone that they consider "more important".

- People who take their leave after discovering that you do not work for a company that they consider useful.

One thing that I've noticed is that people often don't want to admit that the best networking is done by decent, honest, respectful and nice people when they have their own networking demons that they struggle with. If you feel insecure or nervous in a room of people it can be easy to try and demonise "networking" and blame it for your lack of success rather than looking inside yourself and trying some new things. Don't worry if this is you! In the rest of this book we tell you how to network in the best possible way, by being true to yourself and your passions and by being a courteous and friendly human being.

You may perceive an apparent contradiction between this ethic and the strict instructions that you must stop talking to people who are boring you. This is a common thread in business (and in life!). You have a responsibility to be polite and courteous and networking will also work best when you are kind. There is a difference, however, between being kind and carrying someone. We'll talk later in the book about how to help someone by doing something for them that takes around 5 minutes, which is a tip that I learnt from an excellent book called "Give and Take" by Adam Grant. This rule really helps me to distinguish between giving and being kind and over-giving and risking becoming a doormat. You will only increase your networking capability (and potential enjoyment) by spending 5 minutes talking to anyone who would like to meet you. You will ruin your evening by spending the whole night talking to someone with whom you have not made a personal connection.

Being insincere or inauthentic

I am certain that if you are less enthusiastic that me about networking, one of the key reasons is that you have met people who were insincere when you met them. Lack of sincerity can cover a large range: from people who you believe are outright lying to people who simply seem inauthentic – people who just don't seem "right" and you find it hard to trust them.

Similarly the reasons for people acting in this way are very diverse. Although you may come across old school salespeople who not only want to bore you about what they are selling but also want to claim untrue miraculous results for it, I don't believe that this is the main reason that people end up misrepresenting themselves.

A large number of people in the world have a job or

work for a company that doesn't fit with their values. The job is not what they want to be doing, or the company does not quite operate in a way that they believe to be correct. If, like me, you are lucky enough to work for an organisation where you are aligned with their values, and have the potential to change them, you might not realise how difficult it can be for people who do not. It is also the case that people who (for whatever reason) do not feel that they are in a position to leave a company that they hate are likely to also be less confident and outgoing and willing to just put themselves out there.

Imagine that you earn a reasonably living selling accountancy software, which is a job that you fell into by accident. You aren't particularly interested in accountancy, and although there are great people where you work, the culture is one of command-and-control with lots of power resting with those who are more senior than you. Your boss has sent you to a networking event to sell more software and is quite clear that if you don't come back with some sales there will be consequences. How would you behave? Instinctively authenticity and bringing yourself to the party would go straight out of the window.

Another really common reason for people appearing to be pretending is that they mistakenly think that this is how you network. There is a fine line between the technique of "faking it until you make it", which I describe later in the book and pretending to be another person. Because this is such an important topic and one so difficult to apply to your own life, many books and training courses discuss it. One of my favourite descriptions of how to both "fake it until you make it" and retain your authenticity is to "be the best possible you". If you don't like parties, you shouldn't pretend to, but you do need to smile and look your conversation partner in the eye.

I am going to talk next about being nervous leading to bad networking and giving an impression of insincerity can be one of the consequences. Revealing our true selves is a very risky business. If I reveal my dreams and hopes to you, and you are dismissive or critical that can really hurt me emotionally. If I tell you a standard story about how I want to get to the next step in the career ladder, even if you think I am unimaginative and conventional, your criticism cannot hurt me as much because I am only repeating a standard trope. Like a lot of networking skills bringing your true self to the party requires a lot of practice and courage. Don't worry if this is something that you are working on. It is perfectly normal and I will give you plenty of hints and tips for how to do this in the least painful and most engaging way in this book.

Another way that this can happen is when people are inauthentic with others simply because they want to be someone else. This could be for any of the reasons that we have already discussed – they are in the wrong job, they are insecure about who they are or they have false expectations of how to be a successful networker.

If you are new to networking and building people relationships you might not think that this negative "anti-networking" skill is that bad. You can see how being rude, boring or talking too much can damage relationships, but not faking being the life of the party.

The problem is that human beings have really great innate senses when it comes to dealing with other people. Have you ever met someone and instantly disliked them? That's because your subconscious using your gut instincts for making snap decisions has found a reason that you might not want to do business with that person. Gut instincts are not always correct, but they play a big part in how we subsequently go on to deal with people and how much trust and effort we choose to put into the relationship. If your subconscious can't make a whole human being out of the facts that it is presented with you will not have a satisfying conversation. The easiest way to put someone else's instincts at ease is to be friendly, polite and most of all be yourself.

I was recently lucky enough to go and see the fabulous TV show, QI (which stands for Quite Interesting) being filmed. One of my friends who I went with is a software developer and not commonly in a situation where you need to chat with lots of people that you don't know. In the green room afterwards, over a drink or two, we got to chat with the QI elves – the people who research the facts and questions for the show. My colleague found the experience unsettling. "Zoe", he said, "how come these people are both geeky and interested in facts and also shallow and outgoing?".

It occurred to me that this is a common introvert misconception. I believed things very similar when I worked as a software developer at the start of my career. Being outgoing and interested in other people does not automatically make you insincere.

Being nervous

As a women working in the field of technology, I am often invited to events that talk about "women in technology" or "women in business". There are training sessions to help women with particular traits or misconceptions that are holding them back in the careers. One of these ideas that comes up time and time again is Imposter Syndrome.

Imposter Syndrome is a description of the feeling that your current position or respect that people have for you is completely unfounded. It's when you believe that you have got to where you are by luck or by skilful deception – by pulling the wool over others' eyes. If they knew what you were really like, you never would have got that promotion. In short, you feel like a fraud.

Lots of research has been done into the fact that successful women very often feel this way, but research increasingly shows that many men feel it too. I think it is quite a natural artefact of the human tendency to revere and infuse certain roles and positions with a kind of magic. If we grow up believing that to be CEO is an enormous accomplishment that only special people can achieve, then if we reach that level ourselves our own ordinariness (for what is more ordinary than yourself?) will cause a level of cognitive dissonance i.e. we'll have two competing and contradictory beliefs.

The natural human thing to do when confronted with two contradictory beliefs is to discard one of them. Imposter syndrome is where you choose to discard the belief that you have worked hard, built up your skills and earned your position.

Throwing out the other belief instead, that CEOs, pop stars, footballers etc. are all special and magical people is a lot more liberating and, I believe, much closer to the truth. Thinking about Imposter Syndrome in this way has helped me to realise that all people are at times nervous and insecure, even those who appear on the surface to be always confident.

Another common and completely understandable reason for being nervous at a networking event is when you feel that you are inexperienced at networking and don't know what you're doing. You feel that there is a room full of friendly, engaged people who magically know what to do. They are networking people, and you are not. This is a common mistake about almost all talents that people possess, networking especially so. No-one is born knowing how to network. It is a skill that you develop from practice and taking an interest in other people. All the magic networkers are people who took an interest in how to build relationships and learned how to love meeting new people.

Being nervous in all of these situations is perfectly normal and human and for most people passes with time. But it is not "good networking". Imagine if you judged what it meant to be a great footballer by looking at an enthusiastic kid practising on the street, or judged a great singer by her practice sessions. We only see sportspeople and performers who are at the top of their game. When we enter a room full of networkers, we meet the new, the learning and the misinformed. The trick is to find the people who are doing a great job, the people who are having fun and making friends, and to copy what they do.

3

who are you?

We spend so much time talking about our roles and our products that we don't often stop to think about who we are as a person. Good networking is not about roles and it is not about selling. Networking is about people and what you are bringing to the table is you.

This might sound very scary. When I was learning how to network I was shielded from this fact by my mistaken notion (not explicitly taught to me, but one that I incorrectly "worked out") that networking was about selling my business. Given how difficult I found it to go and talk to strangers about what my employer did, talking about myself and what I enjoyed would have seemed like an insurmountable mountain.

And yet… once you start to bring yourself to an event or a meeting, even just a little bit, you start to see the answering spark in other people that you meet. You start to have real conversations and enjoy the experience. This encourages you to reveal a little bit more of who you are and so the process continues. Thinking in advance about who you are and what you enjoy can help to kickstart this process.

You as an individual will also be networking for a purpose. This is fine, and all of the good networkers that you meet will be doing the same. (Anyone who does not have a purpose is not networking, but socialising.) The clearer that you are in what your purpose is (or purposes are) the more naturally and memorably you will be able to explain this to others meaning that you can both maximise your chances of a great connection and also spend the majority of your time talking about other things (i.e. you won't need to over-sell).

On some occasions you will have different purposes. There is an art to both showing up and representing a 360 degree fully formed human being, and realising that at a first meeting you can only show a facet of who you are. You have the power to control which slice of you goes on first display, and you might find that is it not always the one that you are used to presenting.

Confidence in yourself

There are lots of skills that we mistakenly assume are innate when we can all learn and improve at them. I talked earlier in this book about the fact that networking is one of them. Leadership is another. Many people are astonished when I tell them that confidence is also a skill that can be worked on and learned.

Confidence is a combination of knowing what you are capable of i.e. familiarity with the task, and appreciation of the fact that almost everyone else finds it difficult too. There is no better way to build your confidence than through practising and appreciating what you do well. If you are networking at the right places with the right people to learn from, you are likely to feel less nervous than you usually would because great networkers are good at putting people at their ease. I talk about these ways to build confidence more in the section called "Fake it 'til you make it".

One thing that you need to appreciate if you are going to go out and meet people to introduce them to you is that you are unique and special and worth meeting. I find that for so many people who are scared by networking, this is the underlying worry. It is important to remember that your goal is to make real connections, not to please everyone. The fact that you do not "click" with one individual is not an indication that you are doing something wrong, or that you are something wrong. Networkers are not slick talking politicians who are all things to all people. That is the exact opposite of being yourself and bringing what is uniquely you to meet people. A lot of the best networkers are like marmite –

people love them or they hate them.

Revealing yourself can be a process that feels a bit like
you are constructing a character. Thinking about who
you are and what you can offer in various scenarios can
feel calculated and not genuine at all. But everything
takes time and practice (you will hear me say that a
lot in this book!). If you are used to hiding behind a
professional façade, you will need to reacquaint yourself
with who you are and transfer your personal qualities
over into a business setting. It is possible that there are
some aspects of yourself that you will only ever feel
happy sharing with your friends, but the closer you can
get to being the whole you, the easier you will find it to
relate to people.

If you come with your whole personality, you will be
different. There is a myth that in business we should
all imitate each other to the point of looking like cookie
cutter versions of the "executive". Networking throws
aside this myth. It is not how people are, and it does not
help to make business connections.

How to be a real person

One of the earliest lessons that we learn, first in school
and then in business, is to leave our real selves at home.
Personality is not considered an advantage in school

or in mediocre workplaces. This is a travesty! Business consists entirely of making genuine connections with other people – if you leave yourself at home and pretend to be the "generic business person" you will only ever have superficial relationships.

Talking about your interests, hobbies and personality outside of how it applies to your day job is a fantastic networking technique. When you meet new people, you will bond best with those with whom you have something in common. If you introduce yourself as an accountant, they are in marketing and you only discuss day jobs you will both find conversation difficult, painful and likely very, very boring. If you bring other aspects of yourself into the conversation – for example, the fact that you like cycling, the age and challenges of your children and your love of jazz – there is much more chance that you'll elicit a response of "Me too!" from your conversation partner.

One great way to work out what you are about as a person is to make a Word Cloud. This is a really simple exercise, and one that you can repeat every few years if you feel that your old cloud is out of date. Brain storm words that appeal to you or describe your personality, interests and achievements. Make a list of 50. I found that fifty seemed like a huge target to start with, but once I got into the swing of it, I kept thinking of other words that I wanted to include (e.g. "dragons"!). You can see my word cloud at **http://www.zoefcunningham. com/blog/word-cloud**.

Another reason that I love to mention the word cloud exercise is that I learnt it from Glenn Watkins at the Academy for Chief Executives. I hadn't met Glenn before he phoned me up to invite me to the Academy, yet by the end of the session I felt that I knew him really well. One thing that I will always remember is that he loves motorbikes, which means that I think of him as a rounded human being rather than just a businessman.

I read a lot of books about business, life and relationships, which I try to gradually build up into a picture of the world. I've been speaking for a long time on why it's important to bring yourself to the table when you meet new people, but it wasn't until a recent Tech Talkfest networking masterclass that I realised why we find it so scary. The insight came from referencing the great book "Daring Greatly" by Brene Brown.

Brene Brown swept to fame after she gave a TED talk on the topic of emotional vulnerability, which she also covers in her book. Every time you face rejection, you're vulnerable and how you deal with this determines what kind of person you are. If you restrict conversation to your job and the company that you work for, any reaction or boredom, cynicism or disinterest doesn't hurt you personally. But if you've revealed more about you, rejection can be more painful. I think this is worth bearing in mind if you are finding it difficult to open up – it's important to learn how to do so, but maybe try with small steps until you are comfortable.

Know what you're offering and what you're looking for ("elevator pitch")

I talked in the introduction to this chapter about having a purpose for networking. This is an intentionally vague term. Networking to sell a service or product is definitely not the only possible purpose and it this very multiplicity of needs that makes networking so interesting, fun and rewarding.

Some people are networking because they are new to an area and want to make new contacts, both for business and for social purposes. Some people are looking for rare or interesting information that can only be found by meeting other people rather than by using a data search. Recruitment feels like a sub-category of this – if you are networking for recruitment purposes, you are looking to find out who the people are who would make great employees. This information is hard to get in any other way than talking to potential recruits. Business partnerships of all forms can also be best found through networking. For all businesses but particularly for startup businesses, who your suppliers are is as important to you as who your clients are. Every time a connection is made in networking one side wins, and the other side wins too.

It is worth thinking not just about your primary purpose but also about whether there are any other problems that you have that you might be able to solve by networking. Do you need advice? Could meeting a mentor or coach be useful, or could just having a sympathetic chat with a leader from a different industry help you right there and then? It might be worth sketching this out into a mind map or other free form diagram, or using whichever technique you find helps you to be creative. There will definitely be more opportunities here than you have previously considered.

Once you have a good idea why you are networking you need to find a way to make this concise and digestible. Just as with your personality, there will be myriad facets and complexities of why you are networking, who you are looking to meet etc. You need to decide which ones it makes most sense to reveal and work out how to order them into a story.

If you are familiar with sales terminology, you may have heard this process referred to as an elevator pitch. This phrase is derived from the following scenario. Imagine that the person who can grant what you need (money, patronage, contacts or other help) has just got into an elevator with you. Are you able to explain to them, using only the time it will take to get to their floor, exactly what you need and why they should help?

This is a very American scenario, where the salesperson is so concise that they can enter a lift having never met the other occupant and end with a handshake and a signed check. I hope you will already have an idea from this book that real networking does not work like this!

However, thinking about how to be concise about who you are does lead to better connections. Remember the bad networkers that we met at the start of the book? In today's society everyone is busy, and they are themselves networking with needs and wants of their own. Your aim should be to be as courteous as possible and respecting people's time is an important part of that. You are not reeling off a pitch in order to close a quick deal and make a quick buck, but you do need to explain who you are and what you are doing without taking ten minutes to explain the background to your business.

If you are going to networking events, the need to introduce yourself will arise again and again and again – every time you meet a new person, in fact. Time spent thinking about and planning for how you will do this is the best possible way to spend your prep time and will help with feelings of nerves and confidence too.

I find that the easiest way to start is to draft a speech out on paper. Once you are comfortable presenting yourself, you won't need to work from a learned script, but it can be a very handy way to get started. Think of the simplest possible way to describe what you do. Can you do it in even fewer words? Keep refining it until it's as short and simple as you can get. Take care that you don't use any industry specific jargon. You may be used to calling yourself a Change Management Consultant, but will that explain clearly and concisely what you do to someone who isn't familiar with that role? Explain what you do for what kinds of people rather than just stating a title.

While you are starting out at this, grab the chance to ask for feedback! Although you may be worried that people will think less of you if you reveal that you are new to game, the opposite is in fact true. Everyone loves to help out someone who is just starting out, and by letting on that you aren't a seasoned professional you may find you get better help and contacts that you would have done otherwise. So smile after you're done and say something like "Did that sound natural? I'm working on my introduction. What did you understand that I do?". If the answer doesn't match your intention, you get the opportunity to do a little refinement before you meet the next person!

Be memorable

A room full of brilliant networkers is like one giant
information exchange, where the information is all
about people. When I picture a room full of the best
networkers I know it reminds of a telephone exchange
or a computer algorithm. At a high level, every single
person can be considered to be interacting by using the
following steps.

1. Introduce yourself.

2. Find out about the person you are introduced to.

3. Run through every contact you have in your head to
   see whether you know anyone who can help with
   the aim, goal or interest that you have just found out
   about.

4. Find out a bit more about the person you are
   introduced to.

5. Repeat step three.

6. Mentally file the person you have just met, so that
   you can use them for future step threes.

(Steps 4 and 5 can be repeated until you both feel that
you've helped each other as much as you can.)

Whenever you meet someone at a networking event,

the person to whom you are introducing yourself could be one of these super-connectors. If so, you are likely to carry on receiving the networking benefits of having met them once when they go on to other events and make new connections with other people to whom you might be useful. In this case it will be important that you stick in their mind, and also that you're filed under the right categories for the areas that you really need help with.

Being concise and to the point (as well as being respectful of your conversation partner's time and a good weapon against being boring) is a good way to be easily recalled for the right things. If you listed out every function of your business in a long and complicated way, you will likely to filed under "did something to do with business" and you'll either be recalled in the wrong context or, worse, not at all.

It's also worth thinking about any aspects of what you do that fit within a current market need or zeitgeist. I met Katrina and Gloria of the Diverse Leaders Network when I was a mentor at a Launchpad that they were taking part in. I have been able to recommend them much more often than other companies of their cohort because to my knowledge they are the only company addressing this very important area. Their name, Diverse Leaders Network, explains exactly what they are trying to achieve – their aim is to increase the diversity at the top of Britain's businesses, a topic close to many people's hearts. Think about who the people are who you can most help and make that part of your pitch – as with most business interactions it's best to not rely on people reading between the lines. Spell it out for them!

You may be lucky enough to be someone with eccentric dress sense, or a taste for bright clothes. It's interesting that while in many circumstances, particularly corporate ones (!), this can be a disadvantage, in networking it means that you will stand out and be easier to recall. Hooray for individuality! Of course, I don't recommend trying this as a tactic if it doesn't sit well with your personality – remember that being genuine is most important above all else.

Finally, whatever you do and whatever kind of person you are there are two great ways to make yourself engaging and memorable.

First, be enthusiastic. Enthusiasm gets people's attention. If someone is very engaged with the topic that they are discussing, we assume that it must be interesting and listen more closely. If you're out networking and feel the need to talk about topics that you don't feel enthusiastic about, you should consider getting a new job.

Secondly, take an interest in the other person. This

is always a good idea, but especially so for making yourself more memorable. Ask smart, open questions and listen closely to what they do, what circles they move in and what challenges they and their network are facing. That way you can relate what you do to their life and experiences, which will help make sure you're filed in the right place.

Different hats for different occasions

I'm not sure how prevalent this is in other cultures, but in Britain we seem to feel that we are defined by our day job. I know of very few people who don't answer the questions "What do you do?", "Who are you?" or "What's your job?" in that way. Further, many people feel that if they don't answer with their title, company and role description, they are somehow being dishonest or disingenuous. Having spent a long time networking in lots of different environments, I now consider this to be a very limiting concept, for several different reasons.

For a long time, I could only answer the "Who are you?" question with reference to that fact that I worked for a software development company. I was a software developer, or a project manager, or a consultant and I felt that was the only way to define myself. Introducing

myself in this way, I ran out of conversation very quickly.
It also reinforced the idea that if I was at an event,
networking, I ought to be initiating conversations around
software development, and persisting with these even
when the other party was not particularly interested.
Insisting on sticking with one topic meant that I listened
less to the other person, because I had no way to get
involved with their story and their interests.

Now let's imagine instead that I turned up as a whole
human being, with a range of skills and interests. I could
flesh out my introduction to "I'm a software developer,
who enjoys singing classical music and reading novels."
That means that the person I am talking two has three
different places to carry on the conversation. Anyone
who is desperately seeking software developers will
want to talk about my day job. However, anyone who
doesn't have the slightest interest in, or need for,
software development can continue by asking "Ooh,
what music do you sing?" or "Have you read any good
novels recently?".

Even more importantly, let's imagine that I am attending
a networking event related to one of my outside
interests, for example radio presenting. (The excellent
organisation Soundwomen runs many events for women
who work in radio to meet each other, for example.)
If I introduce myself as a software developer in this

environment, the first reaction will be one of confusion. "What? Radio software?".

The tempting solution is to give both answers – "I'm a software developer by day, but I present a radio show for Shoreditch Radio in the evenings." This is better, but you're adding in extra information that almost no-one is going to be interested in. I've never had a conversation about technology at a radio event. Why not instead say "I'm a radio presenter with community station Shoreditch Radio, and I sing classical music and read novels." – three relevant topics that might lead on to interesting conversations. I'd like to clarify that I am not suggesting that you lie or "big up" your role – if you're a volunteer presenter with a community station, say that, don't pretend you're working for Radio 1 – but lead with the parts of you that are apposite for the environment.

Looking even deeper into personalities, I think that even the answer above is over-simplified. You might be a lawyer who loves the "dealing with people" aspect of law. Or you might be an accountant who loves to help people who are struggling with their own business to focus on what really matters while you sort out the numbers for them. You can describe yourself in any of hundreds of ways – try on a few different hats and see what suits you.

fake it 'til you make it

You're almost definitely reading this book because you don't feel confident in your networking skills. I've been there myself. There appears to be a group of people who are confidently meeting people, having fun and getting ahead and you don't feel as if you are one of them. The commonly accepted explanation is that they are naturally vivacious or born "people people". These explanations imply that for some reason or other you can't be as good as them. In this chapter we'll explore the idea that these common explanations are wrong.

When I started networking I would have loved a magic wand that could transform me instantly into one of these happy, smiling confident people. I longed to not feel nervous and inferior. The great news is that using the following hints and tricks you can do exactly that. Remember that when you are looking at other people, you are only seeing their outsides. You can't see in to what they are really thinking. Imagine if these people too were nervous about making a mistake, or saying the wrong thing? It turns out that the secret to becoming one of them is to realise that this is exactly what is happening.

When I was younger I was really struck by the following quote from Eleanor Roosevelt. "No-one else can make you feel inferior, you can only do that yourself." I found it terrifying because it implied that my feelings of inferiority, which I had been blaming on "powerful others" were on the contrary of my own doing and hence my own responsibility to resolve.

The concept of "fake it 'til you make it" relies on an iterative process. When you start to imagine and project that you are a little more confident, gradually you become so. You can then start to project the next level of confidence and once again reality will catch up with you. The more confidence you are able to pretend you feel the quicker this process will be.

How to look confident

I am constantly fascinated by the research done by psychologists and how it often conflicts with what we think are the explanations for how the human mind works. Simple facts about the mind, such as how we make decisions turn out to be not nearly as straightforward as we imagine. The relationship between feeling emotion and showing emotion turns out to be one of these mechanisms that don't work as we expect.

Our usual model for how emotions work is that when someone is sad, they will show this on their face, for example they will cry or become withdrawn. When they are feeling happy, they will smile. Psychologists have shown that this emotional link works both ways. This means that if you smile, you will become happier. Similarly if you frown, you will become sadder.

This fact is one of the central ideas that we can use in our quest to "fake it 'til we make it". By focussing on physically changing ourselves so that we appear to be more confident, we can stop worrying about whether we actually are or not and get on with meeting people and having fun. Not only will we start to feel more confident, we will also look indistinguishable from those special people who are "naturals" at networking.

There are several things that confident people can do that you can mimic.

Smile. Smiling is the most natural and engaging human expression. Confident people smile frequently, which makes those who they are interacting with feel happier and at ease. Practice smiling whenever you can. Smiling shows that you are listening to the person who is speaking and that you appreciate what they are saying.

A particularly great place to start practising smiling is when you are in the audience at a seminar. Human beings respond differently when they are listening in a group rather than on their own. For some reason, although we often smile and nod naturally when a single person speaks to us, we don't feel the same need to do this if we are part of a group. If you have ever spoken in public you will have noticed that very often the audience can seem completely disengaged when you are talking, only to rush up afterwards to thank you for the talk and congratulate you on a job well one. Because it is not a one on one conversation, people don't wear their emotions on their face. I believe that it is this simple fact that unnerves most first time speakers. Used to people reacting when they talk one-on-one to them, being confronted by a sea of blank faces means that the speaker feels that they have failed before they even start. So combine practising smiling with helping out a poor speaker! Next time you are in an audience really focus on showing that you are listening and enjoying the talk. It will be great practice for networking for you, and the speaker will really appreciate it too.

Laugh. Being confident is inextricably linked with having a good time. If you are feeling relaxed you will be better able to enjoy yourself and conversely if you are having a good time you will forget about nerves. Find ways to openly laugh. Tell small jokes and amusing stories.

Laugh at other people's anecdotes. Enjoy yourself. Notice how it makes other people react to you. When you laugh, those around you will have a better time too and will flock to be part of your circle.

Eye contact. Confident people are much better than everyone else at maintaining eye contact. It's become a cliché that you should start a business meeting by looking your colleague in the eye and shaking their hand firmly. It's a cliché because it works. Maintaining eye contact is linked to the next point (being deliberate) – try to own your actions. It's also linked to the first point I made – keeping eye contact with someone who is speaking, rather than looking over their shoulder or around the room, will reassure them that you are paying attention to what they are saying. We all find eye contact so intimidating that many business books have exercises to do with eye contact. Timothy Ferris in the Four Hour Work Week challenges readers to make eye contact with people walking down the street. Why not try it as a practice? I've found that getting up the courage to try things like this in the street with strangers (that you will never see again) can make doing the real thing at an event much less intimidating.

Be slow and deliberate. Rushing is a classic sign of nervousness. Perhaps it's because when we're nervous we think that if we can just get it over and done with

everything will be OK (we can then go and hide back
in our burrow). Practise doing things more slowly than
seems natural when you are feeling the pressure. There
is an amazing side effect of this, which is that you will
have more time to think about what you are doing,
which will reinforce the feeling that you are in control. Try
striding deliberately rather than rushing around.

Prepare

When talking about networking, there are lots of
similarities with public speaking. Almost all of the
headings in this chapter could also be applied to public
speaking. Preparation is an essential part of any activity
where you are going to feel exposed – and (to start
with – until you have made it through successful faking)
you may well feel exposed by networking. You can keep
one step ahead of the game by making sure that you
prepare everything you can in advance, to avoid any last
minute surprises putting you on edge.

1. Where is the venue? Where are you going? Do you
   have the address? How are you going to get there?
   Do you have a map handy in case (horror of horrors)
   there is no internet signal when you get nearby?

2. What is the dress code? It is always worth double
   checking this. I, for one, have caused myself a great

deal of unnecessary stress and awkwardness in the past by not paying attention to this and turning up under- or over-dressed. For dressing for an event, I have some more tips on this in the Networking Events section. If you are meeting someone one on one, try to adapt your dress code to their style. Don't copy their outfits (that would be creepy) but if they tend to be casual tone down what you would usually wear, and if they tend to be smart, pick something from the smart end of your range.

3. Do you have everything you need? Number one thing you need being, of course, business cards. There is nothing more frustrating and more of an obstacle to getting the most out of a networking meeting than failing to take your contact details with you. It's not the end of the world if you do forget them (you might just have to resort to pen and paper), but by just thinking ahead you can save yourself that little bit of extra embarrassment. If you want to be extra prepared, something that I always carry with me is a set of blank business cards, in case other people have forgotten theirs. That way I can just ask them to write their contact details down for me.

4. Have you eaten? Or in some cases, made sure you haven't eaten? I can't count the number of events that I've been to and ended up famished because I

didn't realise that there wouldn't be food. I've also now started making the mistake the other way and turning up full to parties with a large buffet spread. Why not check in advance?

5. Prepare your elevator pitch in advance (see Who are you? section).

6. Finally, if you are really new to networking, you can prepare a list of questions to ask and techniques to start and end conversations. See the Networking Events section.

Practice makes perfect

One of the most perfidious concepts that we have as human beings is that of natural talent. Despite our "natural advantages", whether that's long legs that make you a runner, "pianist's fingers" or some other such physical characteristic, pretty much 100% of the expertise and talent that you will see in the business world is learnt.

I have spent a lot of time training new project managers, and it is incredible to see how people can be intimidated rather than inspired by those with more experience than them. I love telling people that our Operations Director was once a new project manager and made all the mistakes that they are making now.

We are most intimidated by this perceived natural talent when at an event with senior executives who seem completely at home in chatting to others. We look around at a room full of people who are casually making deals, introducing people to useful contacts, laughing and having fun. We are not like that, we think (or at least I certainly have!).

The single biggest secret to everything in life is that practice makes perfect. Whenever you see someone doing something really well, they will have practiced it, very possibly for 10,000 hours (this is the amount of time that it is now commonly accepted that you need to spend practising something in order to become a genius at it). In 2013 I was extremely excited to be selected to talk at TEDxRussellSquare. And also very nervous. TED talks have a reputation for being flawlessly executed, every single one. I felt that I had to make sure that I didn't let the side down. So I practiced my TED talk like I had never practiced a talk before (or, indeed, since). I had a three times a week practice schedule for months in advance of the event. And do you know what feedback I got after that talk? That I was a "natural". This is the principle of practice makes perfect in action.

There are many things that you can practice in advance of a networking event. Practice your pitch. Make sure you know it off by heart. Practice it to the point where because you know the essence of what you are saying so well, you can vary the words and keep it fresh and conversational.

Practice talking to people. Every time you get an opportunity. See what happens when you ask people certain questions – are there ways you can have conversations that make other people more engaged and happier to be talking to you? Can you practice identifying the types of people that you will have good conversations with?

But the most important thing of all is simply practicing networking per se. The more people you meet, the more events you go to, the easier it will become. There is also a brilliant trick that I have learnt as a side effect of this approach. If you need to practice before you can go to a networking event, that means that the first few events that you attend don't count. They are simply practice events. So you can go with absolutely no pressure and no obligations. Your only aim is to practice. That can be quite a fun way to get started.

It's not all about you

I have recently started having acting lessons, which for me is another terrifying departure from my comfort zone – just like when I started networking. My teacher is full of pithy sayings that I find can really help to illuminate the human condition. One is "Nerves are vanity". As soon as I heard this phrase it resonated with me. When you are absolutely terrified, it is all about worrying what other people will think of you. In essence you are nervous because you are thinking about yourself.

This relates to one of my top networking tips. When you meet someone, focus on the other person, rather than thinking about yourself. Instead of thinking "What do they think of me? I must look like an idiot", think about how they are feeling and how you can put them at ease. Find out what they do and what they are interested in. Are they looking to meet certain types of people? Do you have any contacts or knowledge that can help them? Do they have any specific interests? Could you learn something from them by discussing what they are interested in rather than what you would naturally talk about yourself?

It is important to realise that it's not just you who feels nervous or out of place at a networking event. A lovely lady called Susan Kennedy who writes under the name of SARK, wrote in one of her recent books that "no-one feels comfortable at parties". I liked that idea and found it a great relief. The same is true at networking events. Even the most experienced people sometimes feel nervous and out of their depth – sometimes being well

known as an "accomplished networker" can increase
the pressure on someone at an event since you have
more to lose then. And remember that almost everyone
in a room is not an "accomplished networker" they are
most likely an average networker at best, or even just
starting out.

One of the magic things about focussing on putting
someone else at ease is that it will immediately make
you look like you know what you are doing. You will
never run out of conversation, because you will be
deliberately creating it by thinking about what the other
person is interested in. You will be visibly having fun
and enjoying yourself, because you have created the
environment where the person that you are talking
to is having fun. You will swiftly become one of those
groups of people that you so dreaded when you walked
in – people who look like they know each other so
well you can't interrupt them. Except that because
you are the person controlling this group and you are
thinking about how to help others, you can smile and be
welcoming to anyone who looks like they might want to
join your group. Best of all, once you are making a real
connection with someone and doing your best to help
them, almost everyone will immediately reciprocate by
trying to help you back – a much more effective way
of getting results for yourself from networking than by
trying to browbeat people into doing what you want.

5

networking events

For many, many people, the true terror of networking hinges around having to attend a "networking event". Networking events come in a variety of guises. Some could just as easily be classified as work events – a conference, a social work event (these are great for internal networking) or some other industry get together. Some are on that awkward balance between social and networking – usually related to some sophisticated pursuit like fine art, where you get to mix with the great and good. For those who are starting out in networking, there are many events that are set up purely for the purpose of networking and advertised as such – either through a networking organisation or by an interested party (e.g. a recruitment firm or other service provider). For more sophisticated networkers many of the events that they do their best networking at will be purely social. Their aim will be to attend, have a great time and meet new people. Networking doesn't sound so bad when you explain it like that!

It is also worth remembering that while events can be a daunting place to network, they also offer fantastic benefits. The sheer number of people who are around makes it easier for you to find someone you will really click with. People love to network at conferences since high profile business people attend as speakers, and you have an opportunity to meet the people at an event whose PA's won't put your calls through to them. Finally an event brings you together with people with common interests to you – even if that interest is simply networking!

The two key things to remember for getting the most out of networking events are to choose carefully which events to attend (in London you could easily be invited to five events every night, so you can't say yes to everything) and to work on your personal networking skills, covered in the last chapter.

What to wear

What to wear is a classic example of a decision that is both less important than people think, and more important. They key aim when deciding what to wear is to avoid any stress impacting you while you are at the event. You will have plenty of other things to cope with if you are new to networking – remembering your pitch, working up the confidence to talk to people –

and the last thing you want is to have to worry about is that you look less smart (or, in some cases, smarter!) than everyone else. So you should plan ahead and make the best choice you can, but, perhaps even more importantly try to chill out about it once you have made a decision. Even if you wear complete the wrong clothes, the best and most genuine people at an event (i.e. the people that you would really like to meet and make contact with) won't look down or dismiss you just based on what you wear. You could even make the best of your mistake and use it as a filter for seeing who is worth talking to.

So first things first, what is the dress code? It is always worth double checking this. I, for one, have caused myself a great deal of unnecessary stress and awkwardness in the past by not paying attention to this and turning up under- or over-dressed. For some business events where "business attire" or even "formal business dress" is required, you will stick out if you are too casual and wearing a suit is always best. In the past a good rule has been that you could never be too smart, but if you work in a modern industry like technology (like I do) you can actually be too smart – often rooms full of hip young tech founders will all be wearing jeans and you can end up feeling like someone's granddad if you turn up in a suit. There are even private member's clubs (most notably Soho House and it's offshoots) where the dress code of the club is "no suits" i.e. you won't even be let onto the premises if you come straight from a formal meeting. If you are going to an event and you haven't been informed on the invitation what the dress code is get in touch with the event organiser in advance and ask them. They will be more than happy to help – it will only help their event to put all of their guests at ease. If you cannot find any details on the dress code and you cannot get in touch with the organiser for whatever reason, I would recommend wearing what you feel comfortable in. I have to admit that on a general working day I tend to wear jeans. I used to dress smarter whenever I had a meeting, but this started to feel inauthentic to me. So I now have a set of smart tops (shirts, jackets etc.) that I can wear with jeans as a kind of halfway house. This style generally tends to work out well, even if I am often dressed less smartly than the person that I am meeting.

What to do

What to do at an event depends very much on what you want to get out of it. If you have the opportunity, I would say that it is very much worth thinking about this in advance. If it is an event where networking is secondary to another purpose, you may need to focus on that first and network around it as you have the opportunity. Only do this if the event purpose suits your goals though. It is an often repeated maxim that the best networking done at conferences is done outside in the hall while the talks are going on. I have to admit that I am easily distracted by coffee and chocolate biscuits, but taking advantage of the facilities offered at the event can provide a great way to meet people, as other people also congregate there and then you already have an interest in common.

For a smaller evening or breakfast event, a good goal can be just to make one meaningful connection. This takes the pressure off if you are thinking you must rush around the room and meet everyone and also encourages you to focus on having a really good conversation with someone – and will remind you to move on if you're not.

Some people like to take notes when they meet people, so that they don't forget the important things that they have found out. It is great to write things down and remember them but it can be rude or off-putting to take notes while someone is talking to you. My favourite halfway house for while you are learning to network is to focus fully on the conversation while you are having it, and then to take some notes on their business card round the corner once you have finished.

If there are stands at an event, this can be an easy win to meet people, especially if you are interested in their services. It is worth remembering that people who are manning stands usually have a strong goal to meet people who will buy their services, so they may not be the best contacts that you make if you are not a potential client.

Who to talk to

The short answer to the question "who should I talk to? Is everyone and anyone! The best networkers never dismiss anyone that they meet at an event. They are polite, friendly and helpful to everyone. I have made most of my best connections at events with someone that I just happened to bump into. A great example of this is my friend Natalie Waterworth of millennial consultancy Talented Heads. I met Natalie at a breakfast event. We got talking over the pre-meal drinks, only to find that we were also seated at the table together. I hardly spoke to anyone else at the whole event, but it didn't matter because Natalie has been such a super contact, getting me two high profile speaking engagements and even making me home made jam!

However, it can also be good to have some direction in your networking. Have a think about what kind of people it would be useful to meet. Here are some examples for me.

- Clients

- Suppliers

- Partners

- Organisers of the event who know who is there and who you could talk to

- People who are great networkers and have an extensive network

- People who are good fun and you enjoy talking to

- People who have experience in your area and can offer advice

- People who could help someone else you know

- People who know about other great events you could go to

Some events will send you a list of attendees in advance (and you can always ask for one if they don't). If you have access to this list, why not do your homework and start the event with a few ideas for people you would like to meet. Having a task may help you feel less nervous and the introductory sentence "I came to this event because I saw you were here and I'd like to meet you" always goes down well.

How to start talking to people

If networking events are the most nerve-wracking way of networking, then the most nerve-wracking part of the event is when you walk through the door and need to start a conversation. This is such a common place to feel nervous that I still feel it when I walk through the door at an event, even though I have attended hundreds in the past.

Common advice for how to deal with this includes "steeling yourself" and "diving in". While great advice, I have found a more practical way to convince yourself to take the plunge is to have a really good idea what you will say to someone when you start talking to them. To that end, I encourage people to create a list of "conversation starting" questions in advance of going to an event, so that when you need something to say you have it ready. The best list is a personal list that works for you, but here are some examples to get you started.

1. Hi, I'm Zoe.

2. What do you do?

3. Who are you here with?

4. What talks have you seen?

5. What talks are you looking forward to?

6. Who are the most interesting people you have met?

7. Who are you looking to meet?

8. What are you most interested in at this event?

9. What do you do outside of work?

10. Where do you live / where were you brought up?

The first of these is super straightforward. "Hi, I'm Zoe."
A lot of people tie themselves in knots when networking
because they think that they need to do something
complicated and sophisticated. Straightforward is
always good when dealing with people. Be yourself
and do things simply. Some people favour introducing
themselves with their full name (first name and surname).
I tend to alternate between this and just using Zoe,
depending on who I am with and what the event is. Like
with everything I recommend using what is comfortable
for you over "the right way". If there is a connection and
you exchange cards or details, people will find out your
surname soon enough.

I give a lot of talks to software engineers on how to
network. I love doing this because so many of them
are terrified of networking and think it is not relevant
for them. I find so often that they are under the
misconception that networking is something that only
salespeople do. A lot of the questions in my list above

are aimed at finding out information that might be useful to you, or establishing a conversation around a subject that you are interested in. If you are at a conference or some other industry specific event, chances are that the things that you are interested in are the things that the person you are chatting to is interested in. I can't stress enough that the other people at the event may well have all kinds of interesting knowledge that it would be really useful to find out, and that you will miss out on if you sit in the corner looking at everyone over the top of your smartphone.

The last question might seem a bit odd, but you'll find it's a great way to get chatting. I'm not suggesting that you ask someone for their address (that would be weird!) but a great way to get chatting with someone is to establish a common ground. Are they from some-where near to you or near to someone you know? Or, on the other hand, if you fail to establish common ground then you will be learning something new. What is it like to live where they were brought up? Would it be worth you visiting? Why did they move to where you are now?

There are lots of other questions that you can ask that I haven't included because they're pretty straightforward. "Do you know any good restaurants / pubs / things to do round here?" is another great way of finding a mutual interest to discuss and very likely

learning something new and useful at the same time.
It is important to remember that to do networking as
well as possible, your number one goal is to have an
enjoyable conversation and get to know someone, and
vetting them as a potential client or partner should be
secondary to that. So while it is useful to find out what
they do and to look for ways to help them or to work
with them, it's not the only thing to discuss and you
shouldn't be trying to discard someone just because
they are not the exact type of person you are looking for.
You may have other interests in common or they may
have connections that they would be happy to introduce
you to who are more aligned to your business interests.
If you establish a good, genuine rapport with them then
they are likely to do this instinctively. If they feel like they
are just being vetted as a business interest, they will be
more inclined to just not bother.

How to get away

If you attend a networking event and don't know how
to start a conversation, you will have zero conversations
– a clear fail for your objectives. What most people
don't consider is that if you don't know how to end a
conversation then you will only have one conversation,
which unless you got very lucky with who you picked to
approach, might not be much better.

It is so easy to end up speaking with someone who is wittering nervously on, or over-selling themselves or their product and who gives you no easy way to end the conversation. In my early days of networking I spent many an event like this, feeling trapped, unhappy and not listening to the person I was talking to. This is a dreadful waste of a fantastic networking opportunity. Firstly you are not having fun, which should always be part of your goal for networking. If you are not having fun, you are not making the best connections. But, more importantly, you are not achieving any of the things that you set out to achieve. You are talking with someone who isn't in any of the categories on your list and if you stay there all night, no-one would blame you for going home and thinking, "hmm, I don't think I'll bother with networking again".

Before I give you some tips on how to end a conversation, I think it's first worth addressing the point about whether it is OK (or polite or "nice") to want to do so. Being nice is an absolute pre-requisite for being a good networker, but there is a clear line between being nice and being someone else's doormat. You will get the most out of your life by being considerate and giving to everyone that you meet. I am a firm believer in that way of doing business. That does not mean that you should sacrifice your own outcomes to those of other people. There is a brilliant phrase that I shall elaborate on further in the chapter entitled "The magic secret of networking" of "enlightened self-interest". You need to ascertain what you want to achieve in life and then get there by working out how you can help other people at the same time. Sacrificing what you want to what they want will not get you there and, I believe, actually help them less too since you will end up grumpy and not with your heart in it. So on this measurement, yes it is absolutely right for you to end a conversation if it isn't working for you.

Another way of looking at it is to think about how courteous the other person is being. If they are thinking about your interests and trying to make conversation that interests you then my bet is that you won't be desperately trying to get away from them, you will be having a very nice time, thank you very much. If on the other hand they are ignoring what you feel and what you would like to talk about, and droning on about their own product, why on earth should you feel bad for cutting the conversation short and going to talk with someone more polite?

So, on that note, here are some of my favourite ways to end a conversation.

1. I'm going to go and get another cup of coffee.

2. Will you excuse me, I need to go to the loo?

3. Ooh, there's someone over there I really need to meet. Let's catch up later.

4. I need to make a call about now.

5. I met someone earlier who was interested in your services, let me introduce you to them.

6. It's been lovely to talk to you, but I want to meet as many people as possible at this event, so let's catch up later.

I hope that by now you agree with me that the last option i.e. the straightforward one, is the best. You have nothing to be ashamed of in wanting to meet people and talk to a variety of people at an event. Note that this is not the same as, and I am not in any way advocating, the "shake hands, get card, look at title, move on if not important enough" approach. Give people a good chance to explain what they do and establish a conversation, but if it's not working you shouldn't be afraid to move on and there is nothing wrong with explaining that politely. You will not make a connection with everyone – some people you will get on with, some you won't.

Whenever I read a networking book, I find that the "super networker" who is advocating a straightforward no-nonsense approach tends to stop at that point. The straightforward way is best, you don't need to worry about it, so just get on with it. Sitting here in the safety of my armchair, I find it hard to imagine why we need any other way than this. But I can remember, particularly when I was starting out, how terrifying it seemed to say that to someone. You are learning. There is no need to set yourself impossible goals so that you give up – the ability to quietly, politely and confidently explain what you want will come in time. In the meantime the goal is to end the conversation and to that end I advocate using anything that works. Use something that suits your personality. I use the coffee excuse regularly and genuinely, because I almost always want another cup of coffee.

Which events to attend

Not all events are created equal. Events can vary in focus, by the type of people attending, by length, location and what extra facilities they offer. Also, if you live in a large city – I live in London – then you will have the opportunity to attend a staggering number of events, enough to fill every minute of your day several times over. You cannot attend them all, so choose wisely.

One rule covers all events of all formats: try them out! You can make some judgements about an event by looking at it on paper, or by asking for recommendations from others (always a good way to choose anything) but you won't really know whether it is a format that works for you until you try it. One law firm might do a better job of hosting a free mingling event than another. You might find a £30 event that gets you better contacts than a £1000 conference ticket. You might find that some of the events that look great on paper are lacklustre in reality. Go to as many as possible and build up your own picture of what a good event for you looks like. And don't be afraid to say no to events. No-one can attend everything, and if you are tired, cranky and want to get away, you won't be getting the most from the opportunity anyway.

What is your budget to attend events? Events have become a popular way for service providers (recruiters, law firms and so on) to advertise what they do, and many understand that overt selling will put people off and so create a nice environment. If you do not have money to spend on event tickets, these events are a great entry into networking, and you will often get a glass of wine too. If the event host is doing their job properly, there will be a wide range of different types of people there. For example if the host is a law firm, the event will be targeted at potential clients and these will come from all walks of life. You can attend the event and not discuss law at all! My top tip for free events is to look very closely at the agenda for the event. Will there be a speaker? Is the speaker from the host organisation or somewhere else? How is the time divided between speaking and networking? If your goals is networking, I would strongly recommend avoiding events where too much of the time is given over to speakers, especially if they are from the host organisation. You may end up feeling lectured to or sold at, and you will not have enough time to achieve what you want, which is to meet people and have conversations. A short and interesting talk isn't necessarily a bad thing, as it can give you a great way in to a conversation with the other guests.

Another type of free event is that organised by a publically or otherwise funded body. These events can vary greatly in quality. The best are run by people who know what makes a good event, and they are conducted with a clear agenda of giving back, so you are likely to get something useful from them and to meet other great people. Some free events can be very badly run though, by people who don't understand what they are offering and don't understand how to facilitate connections. It may seem like a shot to nothing to attend a free event, even if it turns out to be no good but remember that you are spending your time on this event and you could have spent it on a different meetup, another business task or even on a social event. As you have more and more options for places to go networking, you will come to value your time much more highly than money and a bad free event is not a good deal.

The other option is to attend a paid for event. There are quite a few choices at the £30 or under level. Paying for an event doesn't necessarily mean that it will be good, but if you look for paid events that have been established for a long time that implies that people are going back regularly enough to make the event a success. That's a good sign. The decision between attending a paid and unpaid event might also rest on the kind of people that you are interested in meeting. Most people attending paid events have budget from their company to attend events, so you are more likely to meet business people with serious jobs, but also more likely to meet salespeople who are networking for business development.

The majority of events take place in the evening, but you can attend events at all times of day. Traditional semi-social events need to take place outside the working day, so the evening is the obvious option. More professional events can take place during working hours, particularly if the attendees are likely to be paying with company money. Some of these might be billed more as training or learning sessions rather than networking events, but that doesn't mean that they are not a good place to meet people!

There are a number of events that take place over lunch, especially towards Christmas. Some are concise two hour events where the aim is to eat and get back to work, and some, especially those involving lots of alcohol, can stretch on and take up the whole afternoon. These events that are part work and part social can often be the best places to meet people. Increasingly there are more breakfast events being scheduled at the start of the day. This is my personal favourite time to meet people – either at an event or one-on-one for coffee. I have quite a lot of other engagements in the evening and sometimes I just want to go home and chill out with my husband, and I often don't have time to take a large chunk out of my working day for an event. Breakfast is a great compromise – I can get up just a little bit earlier and get into work just a little bit later. Plus there is always food at breakfast events and often very good food too.

Whether you want to eat or not can be another way of selecting events. I always choose events with food if possible, especially in the evening, since I find that once I have committed a couple of hours to going out it doesn't leave much extra time for eating. However I know that people with families would often rather eat at home, so events that start straight after the working day and finish early, or events that are just drinks receptions can work better for them. Events with food can often have more expensive ticket prices, especially in London where a meal out is not cheap.

One type of event that almost deserves a whole section on it is the industry conference. This is a lot of people's networking venue of choice. There are many good reasons to go to conferences, and this is then self-reinforcing since these good reasons attract other great people to network with. Conferences are often sold as primarily a knowledge sharing forum. If you want to know the latest in your industry, you need to attend. There is always a line-up of speakers, often people that everyone at the event would like to hear from – which is of course why it is more effective for them to speak to a large group at once than to everyone individually. Some speakers are those who want to get their own message (usually about their products or services) out to a large group of people and they can take paid for speaking slots. Larger players tend to sponsor conferences and take a keynote speech or other opportunities as part of that.

The success of a conference often rests on the quality of the speakers. Simply put, potential attendees look at who is speaking at a conference and decide whether or not to attend based on that list. Either they are intentionally aiming to try to meet the speakers, or they are internally thinking that they want to meet people like those speakers and so this seems like a good place to do so. If there is someone that you are keen to meet at a conference that you are attending then I do recommend that you take advantage of the opportunity. Bear in mind though that lots of other people will have the same idea as you. As speakers end their talks they are often mobbed by people trying to chat with them – if you are not a pushy type you might not even make it through to say hello. This isn't the only opportunity you have to connect though. I have made great connections by emailing speakers after a conference and saying "I saw you talk and thought it was great. I was hoping to have a chat and didn't manage to catch you – would you be available for a call or coffee?" It's also important not to be that type of bad networker who only thinks that the speakers are worth talking to. It can be great to make connections with the other people who are waiting to talk with a speaker while you are waiting.

Conferences have another advantage. If you are active in your industry then you are likely to meet other people that you know there. Maintaining connections is as important as making new ones and can help the event to feel fun rather than daunting. If you don't yet know the key players in your industry, now is the time to get to know them!

Finally the sheer number of people at an event means that there are loads of opportunities to meet all kinds of interesting people. Some you will be able to help and some will be able to help you.

On the note of becoming reacquainted with people that you have already met, there are quite a few events that run as a series or are run by a community of people. I find this is the best way to make the best type of contacts – those that start to cross over the line from "contact" to friend. Networks like the Byte the Book hub for digital publishers run monthly events. I love going to a Byte the Book event because I know that there are likely to be at least half a dozen people that I can have a really great conversation with – we have done all the small talk of finding out who each other is at a previous event. Ada's List is an online email group for women in technology (there are lots of these groups – more on that in a minute) with monthly coffee mornings. Having been to a few of these mornings already, they are now a perfect mix for me of friends I can say hello to unselfconsciously and new contacts who will be my friends of the future.

So just quickly on the topic of women's networking groups – there seem to be more and more of these springing up. Whether or not you believe that there ought to be a need for such groups, if you are a woman it can be worth trying a few of them out. (A large number of these groups are open to men too. I've never seen one from that perspective, but I can imagine it can be worth a go to go along as a man and be in the minority – you'll have that advantage often cited by successful women of being more memorable simply because you're in a minority.) I've found that senior women at women-focussed events are always super helpful and will go out of their way to find connections for you. I think this is another case of being on common ground – other groups that might have a similar atmosphere could be LGBTQ groups or school, college or other alumni groups.

One type of event that I have found less successful is the more formalised networking association, such as BNI. These tend to be no-nonsense, target focussed affairs, which I find quite destroys the kind of vibe that I am looking for when I network. In the chapter "The magic secret of networking" I go into more detail on how you get the most from your network by looking to give to others, without expectation of return. BNI have taken this idea and turned it into the rather alarming "giver's gain" creed whereby everyone is expected to produce leads (not just helping contacts or potential friends) to others in the group, and these are formally accounted and displayed as charts! It was after attending one of these events that I realised how networking has managed to get such a bad name. Whereas these type of events are obviously successful for a lot of people, if you are starting out I recommend that you focus on events that are fun and welcoming so that you learn to love, rather than fear networking.

As you become a more successful networker, you will start to be invited to exclusive invite-only events. Some of these will not be as exclusive as they seem, "invite only" can sometimes just be a way to get you to turn up. (However, once you know this you can use it to your advantage – if you hear about an invite-only event that you would like to go to, try emailing the organiser to ask for an invite. More often than not you will get one!) And don't forget that just because something is exclusive doesn't mean that it is any good. Having said that, a curated guest list and an incentive to the other attendees to turn up (because it is exclusive) can make for the best kind of networking. I tend to err on the side of accepting these invites, at least for the first time. If nothing else I find it interesting to see how other events are organised and what things encourage others to attend.

A place that I think should be great for networking and sometimes isn't is the private members or gentleman's clubs. (If you are from America, note that I do NOT mean strip clubs.) These venues collect groups of like-minded people and have a common meeting place to boot – they should be perfect. I think that one of the issues is that the clubs focus on famous people, who are easily identified and often don't want to be surrounded by a coterie of admirers. So it's not usually accepted to just start chatting to people, and you may be disappointed if you join a club in order to meet different types of people. Two exceptions that I know of are the Hospital Club, which has an online system that you can use to contact any member, and the Union Club in Soho where we at Exponential are running a network to connect members within the club.

Finally don't forget that you can make useful connections wherever there are people. A lady that I used to work with (she was Head of Business Development), used to always come back from holiday with several new connections and parties can be a great place to meet people. If you have to attend a social event where you don't know people and where you would usually feel awkward, why not out your networking questions from earlier in this chapter? You might even end up having more fun.

meeting one on one

Going to networking events is a good way to meet lots of people at once, but the best way to really get to know someone is to meet them one on one. There is no substitute for this. It's not always easy to find the time, especially when you have a full time job to do, and it gets harder the more connections you make and the more invites you get.

Meeting new people over coffee has become my favourite way to network. I would take it over an event any day. The atmosphere is relaxed, it's easy to focus on the person you're talking to and you can choose where to meet, which means that the coffee is usually better too. I've made some brilliant connections – TV executives, UKTI mentors, network founders – simply by getting in touch with people I'd like to meet and asking them the magic question "would you mind meeting for coffee?".

As my profile has grown through public speaking and TV and radio work, I now find that I have more people coming to me to ask me if I would like to go for coffee. This can be slightly daunting to start with, but luckily I'm not yet at the position where I don't have time to say yes to the requests I get. I have been absolutely amazed by the great connections that I have made this way. I've met loads of entrepreneurs with great businesses and fantastic energy and they will be fantastic contacts for me for the future.

Can we meet for coffee?

Think of someone you'd like to meet. Maybe someone senior in your company who could make a good sponsor or mentor for you? Maybe someone in an organisation that you hope could become a client of yours one day? Maybe someone whose career you have admired from afar and who you would love to ask how they did it? Now pick up your phone, or open your email, and ask that person for coffee.

This can feel extremely daunting when you are starting out. Why would they want to speak with you? Aren't they far too busy and important to spend time talking to you? Well as it turns out, most often, no they're not too busy. One of the most amazing things that I have discovered as a result of doing extensive networking is that the more successful people are, the more they are willing to give back and help someone else out. Everyone who is really successful knows that this is how it works. They know this because when they themselves were starting out, someone went for coffee with them and helped them on their way.

This approach won't always work, but you have nothing to lose by trying. Another thing that we often worry about is that we will look forward, or be annoying or somehow cause ourselves problems if the person we get in touch with doesn't want to have coffee with us. Provided we are polite if they say no (it's not OK to keep contacting them if they don't want to see you!) we can only gain by trying to meet with someone. They may be too busy to even reply to your email, but your name may stick with them for the future, for example if they are on the lookout for bright young things within the organisation.

As a back of the envelope calculation, I think I have managed to meet or have a call with maybe 25% of the people that I have got in touch with. And when I've managed to meet with people who didn't get back to me, I've realised that they're never the best contacts anyway. If you are looking to make genuine connections, you are much better off meeting the people who are happy to spare 30 minutes to help someone else, rather than someone who is only interested in what you can do for them.

One group of people that this approach is less likely to work with is those with extremely high public profiles, for example actors or TV personalities. While they too, as successful people in a very competitive field, are very likely to be lovely people who would be delighted to help, unfortunately as they become better known they tip over to the point where they get so much incoming contact that they can't process it all and stay sane. In some cases, if they had a public email address and opened it when they got up and processed emails until they went to sleep again, they literally could not read them all. People in this situation have agents to filter their emails for them, and while they would be likely to want to help you, sadly their agent is not going to feel the same way. The good news is that the people with a public profile are very rarely the best people to meet anyway. If you were interested in talking about TV motoring shows, the producer of Top Gear (see, I suspect you don't even know their name) is likely to be a better contact that Jeremy Clarkson.

Get an introduction

If you feel uncomfortable cold contacting people, which a lot of us do, it can be easier to get in touch with someone if you have been introduced. Introductions form the backbone of networking.

In an ideal world, we would all live within five minutes of each other and be at the same events. In this situation I am sure that in person introductions would be the most popular way to meet people. In reality it is rare that you will be in a room with a person you know and the person they would like to introduce you to. So most introductions are done via email.

The email introduction is an art form in itself. Now that I have done a lot of introductions by email, I have found that certain things make for better connections than others. First, I explain who both parties are. Not a long biography but enough so the other person can get a handle on what they are about. Sometimes one or other of the people I am introducing may have asked to be introduced to the other one, or I may have already explained who they are in which case I skip one half of this.

It is not always necessary but I also like to suggest what the two connections have in common, or could do together and what they might like to do as a next step e.g. "maybe you two could grab a coffee together?". Without this, sometimes people can be confused about why you are introducing them. One lady I know is a great introducer, and does so simply on the basis that the two of you "might get along". Someone that she introduced me to in this way responded to my friendly follow up by saying that she didn't think we had anything in common and she wasn't interested in meeting with me! I am not sure what my friend had in mind when she introduced us, but perhaps if it had been clearer to this other lady she may have taken the connection rather than dismissing it.

As I mention many times in this book, we are all busy, busy, busy. Some people will take a connection that you make for them on trust, but others with so much to squeeze into their calendar need a little more convincing.

Another way that I like to soften what would otherwise be a cold contact is what I call the "half introduction". This is when someone has recommended that you talk to someone they know (and possibly also given you their contact details) but hasn't done a formal introduction. These are the emails that start "Mary recommended that I get in touch with you because…". I find that even without the email coming from Mary (or whoever), a common connection helps people to place you and makes them more likely to want to help.

The great thing about introductions is that while they are a great way to meet people and start networking, they also allow you to continue networking by then introducing the person you have met to other people that they might find useful. The circle continues.

Meeting or phone call?

Sometimes when you ask someone for a coffee, they will offer you a phone call instead. Provided you have offered to go to meet them where they are based (which you should do! See next chapter) a call does not save much time over a coffee. However, for a lot of people it can make them feel safer when they don't know you, in that they can end the conversation more easily and perhaps feel that they need to commit less.

Personally I always prefer to meet in person where possible, so if given the choice I would choose a meeting, but it's important to work to the other person's agenda if they are doing you the favour. It is better to thank them politely for offering to give up any of their time at all for you, rather than sounding disappointed that they won't meet.

Calls can also be a fabulous way to catch up with people who are located on different continents, either permanently or temporarily. I've often first "met" someone who is away on business via a phone call, which can be followed up in person when they are back.

Skype is also now a brilliant option, halfway between

a call and a meeting. You can really feel like you've met someone properly over a Skype call. I had a very strange experience once at an event where I met someone that I knew but he seemed to be taller than he used to be. It was only then that I realised that I'd only previously spoken to him by Google Hangout, rather than in person!

Where to go

When deciding where to meet, there is an unwritten rule that it is important to respect. If you are contacting someone and asking them to meet you, you should offer to meet at "theirs" whether that is their offices, a coffee shop near their house or some other convenient location for them. Do not contact someone, ask them if they can very kindly spare 30 minutes and then expect them to travel to you! Similarly if people contact you, you should not feel bad for asking them to come to you. Often I can fit in a quick 30 minute meeting at my offices in Kentish Town that would be completely impossible if I needed to travel into the centre of town.

You might find that some people are more flexible in terms of where they can meet, so even after you have offered to come to them they may be happy to meet in the middle, or near to someone else where they have a meeting. I have a list of favourite places that I use for various times of day: good places for breakfast, places with high quality coffee, quick lunch venues and best of all a café/bar that is perfect for 5pm meetings as we can have coffee or a glass of wine depending on the person I am meeting.

You may also be concerned about what to wear when meeting someone new. My advice is the same as in the networking events section; wear what you are comfortable with, maybe on the slightly smarter side and don't worry too much about it.

Do they like me?

I can plot all of my initial one on one meetings on a scale from "Great! Will stay in touch" to "Oh dear, not likely to contact again". This is perfectly normal.

When you are starting out in networking, or in your career or anything else, it can seem terribly important for everyone to like you, especially the right sort of people, the "good contacts" that you are making. Well, you can accept now that this is not going to happen and you will do better at networking if you don't try to force it.

Your aim is to form genuine connections with people. Some people are looking for people that they can call friends. It needn't be that strong, but you are looking to meet people that you get on well with and would be happy to meet again. People where if you saw them at an event, you would immediately smile and feel pleased to go and catch up with them. If you are not selective about who these people are, you are not forming connections, you are just adding people to an address book.

Even if you are convinced that you have got on brilliantly, you may not end up staying in touch with someone. Again, this is perfectly normal, part of the ebb and flow of life. Keep meeting new people and staying in touch where it happens naturally and you will soon start to see the benefits of being well connected.

Tips for the meeting

So you've sent your tentative email, got a response and booked a coffee. Now what do you do? It's important to remember that this isn't a formal business meeting; you don't need an agenda. Some of the best outcomes for me from informal coffee meetings has been when I know so little about the other person that I can't make a judgement in advance about what a good outcome would look like.

So first up, be genuinely interested in what they are up to, what kind of person they are and what they are interested in. Try to adapt the pace of the meeting to how they are happiest – some people like to rattle off ideas and are happy explaining every little detail of what they do, some people might be happier with a softer approach.

If there's something you are specifically interested in, then do of course mention it – you don't want to get home and be kicking yourself, or to meet up with your new contact a year later and for them to say "oh, I didn't know you were interested in that, I could have introduced you to someone…".

One thing that is worth doing whenever you meet someone is to try and find a way to help them. I talk about this more in the "Magic secret of networking" chapter, but in a nutshell, try to look for things you can do that will help them out – usually this will be something along the lines of a connection. Maybe an introduction to someone you know who provides a service that they need, or maybe you can tweet something that they need promoting? Some people won't be geared up to let you help them if you have called to ask them for help, and don't be alarmed if there isn't a match to be found. Sometimes it will work, sometimes it won't. If you try to help but there is nothing you can do, you have lost nothing, whereas you can seriously impress someone by turning up to a meeting where they expect you to just be asking them for things and instead being full of energy and helpful ideas. (I know this is possible, because lots of people have done it to me and made a big impression!)

It's great to bring energy to the meeting but it's important to remember one basic rule of meetings. I learnt this rule as a manager and I was astonished by the difference it made. Make sure that you don't talk too much. It is so common when you feel that you need to "carry" a meeting, or achieve an objective or make someone feel at ease to try to do these things by talking non-stop. You can end up explaining simple points at length, and cutting over answers in order to ask more questions. Don't do it! Gaps in conversation are usually time when the person that you are talking to is thinking, and thinking is great news. I have found on many occasions that when I have paused for breath I've found that my colleague has been thinking of ways to solve by problems for me, unprompted. Don't take that opportunity away from them.

Don't forget to take a note of any actions that you have promised to deliver. As with taking notes at events, you don't want to overdo this but you will miss a chance to stay in touch if you forget to do what you say you will, so you will need to draw a balance. I find that the most unobtrusive way to take notes is in an old fashioned paper notebook – for some reason writing with a pen seems less jarring than typing into a device. However I can't bear for all my actions not to be connected up, so even though I think it is less ideal, I take notes into my phone or iPad. I often have to explain that I am listening and that I'm taking notes and not checking Twitter.

Staying in touch

Staying in touch after the initial meeting can also be a challenge when everyone, everywhere whatever role they are doing, is always so busy. Keith Ferazzi has loads of great tips for this in his book "Never Eat Alone". I talk more about his book in the Further Reading section, but for now here are two standout ideas from him.

The first one is this. Keep a rolodex (or nowadays, a mobile phone contacts list) of all your contacts and where they live. Get in touch when you are nearby and see if they have time to meet up. Give people a call when you are in a taxi travelling between meetings. I like this as an idea, although I rarely act on it since I don't think I am as well travelled as Keith – I am usually in London, and so can easily meet the people who also live there and rarely am in the same place as those who live outside. I do try to encourage people who come into London to let me know when they are in town, as I can often rearrange things in order to catch up with them. What is so great about this tip is that it gives you a pretext for a quick catchup – even if the person you call isn't free to meet, calling to show that you thought of them is a great way to reinforce the link between you.

The second tip also works along these lines. Nowadays we are constantly reading news articles online or hearing snippets of information. Keith Ferrazi suggests that when you read something that reminds you of someone you know, or is something that you think they might find useful, you forward it on to them. When I first started to do this, I found it a bit clunky and weird. Why would the recipient think I was sending this? Would it look forced or contrived? Much like a lot of other networking tips, now it has become part of what I do I find it really easy. The trick is to not contrive things or to try and make a connection where one doesn't exist. Things we read remind us of people all the time – just notice when that happens and send a message.

Getting in touch with people to remind them that you exist can be an extremely potent tool. Many a time I have contacted someone and they have said "ooh I have been meaning to email you" and they have subsequently made some connection or sent me some useful information that otherwise would have slipped their mind.

online networking

The internet and constant connectivity has brought challenges – the average person checks their phone over 150 times a day and digital addiction is a real issue – but also allows us to connect and expand our horizons like never before.

It also means that we have to ask the question, "What is our network in a digital age?". We are connected to more people in more ways than ever before. So who is part of our network? Our colleagues and associates, for sure, but what about people that follow us on Twitter but to whom we've never spoken? What about the people we follow on Twitter?

Like with the classic tendency of people to feel that they need a "home" personality and a "work" one, many people try to create a different persona for themselves online. Young people growing up with Facebook try to curate their image, leading to an escalating war of who can appear to have the most perfect life. This is an unnecessary complication and the best networking is all about simplicity.

In the same way that people can tell when you meet them if you are being natural and genuine or if you are trying to put on a front, inauthentic online communications are easily seen for what they are. Your aim in everything should be to be yourself – in this vein, your online network is simply an extension of your real world one. There will be some cross-over between the two, and the ease of communicating online means that you can reach more people in our hyper-connected world.

Don't fall into the other trap though – thinking that you can replace real world communication with online updates. Face to face networking is still the best way to make new connections, by a long way. Once you have met someone a few times in the real world it can be easy to feel that you are up to date with what they are doing by simply following them online, but you won't be able to get to know someone for the first time this way. Your aim should be to use online networks to supplement your real world connections, not replace them.

Different sites, different you?

The fact that several competing social media sites can exist at the same time is testament to the fact that they serve different purposes. LinkedIn is very much a business site – no beach photos in bikinis there! Facebook is at the other end of the scale, with students finding on application to university that they should perhaps not have been as free with their profile, or at least should have learnt how to work the privacy settings. Twitter can be used as either, or anywhere in between and not many people know what Google+ is for.

So given these competing forums, should you be tailoring what you post for each one? Well, that depends. If you are keen to share photos of your children with relatives on Facebook then you probably don't want to use that for business. Any network that you keep private like this, you can treat accordingly. But even Facebook can be useful for connecting with people for professional reasons – often if you connect there people feel more like they are seeing the "real you" than if you only show them your CV of achievements on LinkedIn. I have met people who seem to only connect on Facebook, and if I kept my account private I wouldn't be able to keep in touch with them.

Excepting any private accounts, you should aim to be the same person across all of your online touchpoints. I often look at someone's social media accounts to get a feel for who they are, simply because they are often the first results returned on an internet search.

Linking in

It is rare nowadays to come across a serious professional, especially one who is keen on networking, who is not signed up to LinkedIn. When LinkedIn first started, there was a lot of suspicion around it. A Facebook for work? Who would need one of those? Yet, now it is well established there are several features that I find irreplaceable.

The main use that I make of LinkedIn is as a giant personal phone book. Keeping contacts up to date in my own phone is not easy, and I don't really have time (or to be fair, the inclination) to type details out from business cards when I receive them. In our technological era, many solutions to the seemingly antiquated system of passing around pieces of paper with our contact details have been suggested from a unique code that identifies you to an app that can read in details from a card if you just scan it, but I have found none of these as easy to use as the tried and trusted business card method. By just typing in someone's name from their card to LinkedIn and connecting, I can keep track of their current contact details, even if they change phone number or email address. I can also message them through the system. This isn't quite foolproof as some people who don't keep LinkedIn up to date have an old email address configured that they don't check very often, and some people (annoyingly!) don't share their phone number on LinkedIn. But by and large it works pretty well, and for a minimum of effort.

The most popular use for LinkedIn is to cold contact people. LinkedIn works brilliantly for this. Email has become devalued as a way for making contact with people, as companies can put together mass mailshots and send them out to all and sundry. This association with email can mean that sometimes even a personal email is discounted because the inbox is full and it looks like spam. If you have a paid for LinkedIn account, you can send a certain number of introductory messages to other users. However even if you don't have a paid account, you can send a message to someone in a connection invite. This is a great way to introduce yourself, as the message must have been written individually, plus your background and CV is available to read – it is clear who you are as a person. Because you can see someone's background, and a photo, being contacted on LinkedIn (provided that they have also included a good introductory message – always do this if you are connecting to someone you don't know!) feels a lot more like meeting someone personally, and people are correspondingly more likely to respond.

A more recent addition to LinkedIn is the concept of a news feed. You can see article written by your connections, or status updates and links, shared in a feed in a similar way to Facebook. While I don't read this religiously (there are not enough hours in the day!) I find this news feed to be a good way to be reminded of contacts that I met once or twice a while ago, and to keep in touch with what they are doing. The emails that LinkedIn sends with details of who has moved jobs are similarly great for keeping up to date with people.

Having never moved jobs, I don't have any personal experience of this primary function of the site, but a place where connections of connections can see your full CV can only be a good thing. The other feature that I don't think I've used enough on LinkedIn is the "Get introduced" option. In the same way as with an email introduction, coming "recommended" from a shared contact is a great way to meet someone for the first time.

If you are using LinkedIn, it is important to keep your details up to date, and to curate a well-written profile. LinkedIn has many sub-optimal features, one of which is that it creates a whole load of fake accounts for people whose email address it knows, but who are not yet signed up. If you do not upload a photo you risk looking like a fake account. Also even if there weren't such accounts, we instinctively trust an account without a photo less – so you may be missing out on connections if you don't put one up. Make sure it is a good size – whenever a site uses only a thumbnail photo, it's important that your head fills the square (rather than, say, a full length photo) otherwise people won't be able to recognise you. By the same token, use a recent photo and one that is a good likeness.

You do not need to upload details of everything you have ever done to LinkedIn, as some people seem to, but make sure that your career history is clear. As with a CV try not to leave unaccounted for gaps – it will make people wonder what you were doing in that time. If you have several interests or career areas (like me) then you will need to decide whether to focus on one of these or have them all accessible. Since people can find me on LinkedIn from all kinds of different angles, I like to keep all the information on my profile (e.g. my presenting and blogging credits), while setting the main focus to be my executive role at Softwire, since this is why most people will be looking for me there.

One of the most interesting features of LinkedIn is the way that it allows you to see who has been looking at your profile. I find this feature fascinating! Often there is an obvious link to why someone has viewed my profile, e.g. if they have just sent me a message, but sometimes people I don't know seem to look at it and then not contact me at all. My favourite is when I can see that someone I know has looked at my profile and then a few days later I get a request or an introduction from them – aha I think. From the other angle, this can be a terrifying idea if you are just pootling around to look for potential connections. What will all these people who I am viewing think of me? If you like, you can turn off your profile and be seen as just "someone in the IT industry" or similar. I think this is a shame. I refuse to do this because I believe that I shouldn't do things that I'm not prepared to own up to – if I'm looking at someone's page, why shouldn't they know about it? I've actually ended up using it to my advantage too, if I am not sure whether to connect to someone after I have viewed their page, I usually do since it allows me to send an explanatory message ("I was looking at your profile and thought I'd better connect so you didn't think I was stalking you.") This usually seems to go down well.

LinkedIn offers several options if you upgrade to a paid-for account. This will give you the ability to send messages and to see a fuller history of who has viewed your profile. I don't find either of these options to be very useful. Too many people have their profile switched off for a larger history to be useful, and I can send messages via invites. As a free tool, LinkedIn is perfect.

Tweeting

I find Twitter to be a very polarising paradigm. Millions of people are addicted to the short form updates and prefer it to any other social network, whereas others "can't see the point" and bemoan the loss of proper writing skills.

I find that I can't attend a management training course nowadays without someone exhorting me to be on Twitter. It is your public face. It is a way to reach new customers and potential employers. You must be on Twitter if you want to be taken seriously.

Like a lot of modern essentials, I am pretty sure that Twitter is nowhere near as essential as the marketers would have you believe. You can be a very high profile senior executive and go nowhere near it.

That's not to say that it can't be useful, and I think it is worth at least considering whether it would work for you. One thing that Twitter does impeccably is to give you a personal voice. A well written Twitter feed is not a list of press releases from your employer. It is a well-rounded stream of things that interest you: some from your day job, no doubt, but also from your other interests and activities. For me this is a great example of the "be a whole person" motto. You don't need to be simply a professional talking head on Twitter. You can connect with people who match up with different and varied parts of your life.

Twitter also doesn't need to take a long time to maintain. Because of the 140 character limit, the style is to dash out a quick update, rather than crafting a careful piece of prose. Whereas blogging can be extremely time-consuming, especially if you are ambitious enough to try the SEO-maximising challenge of blogging every day, putting a couple of updates on Twitter can take you less than 5 minutes a day. The real challenge with Twitter is to make sure that you don't become addicted to reading other people's tweets and checking for notifications from new followers or retweets of your own posts. I had to uninstall the Twitter app from my phone when I realised how much time it was soaking up – now I only go to the site explicitly in a browser and I find it much safer.

Facebook... for work?

I know that many of you will respond to the idea of using Facebook for work with horror and that is OK. If you really want to keep your account private, there is no reason why you shouldn't do so. The reason that I mention the idea of using Facebook for work in this book is that I think so few people realise that it is possible and haven't even considered whether they would like to do so or not.

Using Facebook for professional as well as personal connections also fits with one of my favourite concepts of networking. You are a single person. You are not a work person and a home person. There are not bits of you that are safe for work and bits you need to hide behind firewalls. I am also a believer in not doing things that you are not proud to display. I don't personally feel the need for a stream of drunken photographs that I wouldn't want my colleagues to see.

I mentioned that some people still don't use LinkedIn for professional connections. These people often will connect to you on Facebook instead. I know people, particularly those who travel extensively internationally, who only use Facebook to communicate. If you are keeping your Facebook as a "personal only" account, you will miss the chance to connect to these people. You will also have other challenges when life doesn't sort itself neatly into boxes for you. What about your brother-in-law who happens to work in the same industry as you – personal or professional?

One way to use Facebook in a professional capacity is via groups. Groups allow you to link people with a shared interest together, what better way to find and support potential clients? Several organisations I know use this to allow their members to talk with and support each other, giving them all a benefit of being part of the organisation.

The other way is to set up a page for your organisation. This is similar to a user account, except that pages are "liked" rather than connected to. Anyone who likes your page will receive updates from it. Lots of companies, especially consumer brands, now have Facebook pages and many use paid for Facebook advertising. As a company Facebook's primary revenue model is from advertising and unfortunately this has affected the efficacy of simply running a page and sending out updates. Updates from pages are deprioritised over updates from regular users, unless you pay to "promote" them. Paid-for Facebook advertising is now a serious option for many businesses, but remember that you might get just as much value if you use your personal account as a networking tool.

Google Plus

There is now a fourth player in the social network field. Having seen the success of Facebook and Twitter, Google made a concerted effort to build a network to compete. They had an inbuilt advantage in that everyone who was already using their email service (quite a few people!) could be conscripted across to the new network.

Some people swear by Google Plus. It is not as limiting as Twitter, or as frivolous as Facebook. Having come onto the scene later than the early services, it seems to more comfortably straddle the gap between a professional service and a personal one.

I have found it difficult to get to grips with, so if you were looking for Google Plus tips, this is not the book for you. I have an account (in fact I have several, since I have more than one google email address and there doesn't seem to be a good way to coalesce them into one account) but you won't see many updates from me.

One feature that I have found useful is the Google hangout. Google's answer to Skype, it does the job well for connecting up to ten participants. Further it has an additional feature that allows you to broadcast your hangout to an audience (Hangouts On Air) – allowing you to become a webinar host.

Minimising the impact

If you are feeling a bit overwhelmed by all these new sites that you need to register with and post updates on, that is perfectly reasonable. Social media is not the purpose of your life, and shouldn't even be the main focus of your networking. (Remember: face to face is always best!)

Given this it is important to focus on a manageable number of services. Some people, especially social media advisors (!) can manage to post on everything, retweeting happily and making it look like a breeze. This is not as easy as it looks, and unless you want to train yourself to move into it as a career I recommend finding the networking tools that work best for you and sticking with them.

I use LinkedIn as an address book (I rarely post or read updates on there), Twitter pretty regularly and Facebook only occasionally. So I usually spot important things on Facebook but often not until a few weeks after they were sent to me.

There are also a few shortcuts for updating your profiles. Tools such as Hootsuite allow you to schedule your tweets in advance, so you can look like you are updating on a regular basis, rather than all in one go. Similarly Buffer allows you to enter several tweets at once and it will spread them out for you.

The other option if you are using Twitter and Facebook is to cross post from one to the other. You can configure your Twitter account with your Facebook login so that your tweets are posted to Facebook. You can post tweets to your user account or to a Facebook page if you prefer.

Forums and mailing lists   .

Yet another way to end up accidentally spending too much time online is to sign up to a forum or mailing list. I'm now a member of several lists where the members can post to all other members by email. Most of them are hosted by Google Groups, which is a great piece of software. You don't need to receive all emails as they are sent – you can receive a digest email instead. I have moved some of my subscriptions over to digest, and eased the burden on my email inbox a little.

The reason that I mention these groups is that I have found them to be very effective forms of networking. By signing up to a common interest list you show that you have something in common with others. Most lists have been established for people to help each other (the whole point of networking, remember) and so I have received free services, helped people to beta test exciting new apps, asked for feedback on my own ideas and even received free coffee for my office!

Like with everything, not all lists will be as good as others. Try them and see if you are getting enough useful information and contacts versus time spent on extra emails. If they don't work – it is easy enough to unsubscribe.

Face to face... online

Science fiction is well known for making many classic booboos when predicting the future, but one thing that most scifi books correctly predicted was the rise of the video call. While perhaps not as ubiquitous or as flawless as once imagined, services like Skype and Google Hangout are now an essential part of the business environment.

How often you choose to use Skype instead of a phone call will vary according with the tastes of the people that you are speaking with. Having used Skype in the early days of poor connection and crackling, I tend to go for a reliable voice call over a risky video conference, but as internet speeds become more consistent and the technology ever better I may switch over. There are already a few uses of Skype that I find invaluable – the great charity Apps for Good arranges for experts in the industry to help review teams of schoolchildren's ideas for apps for the future. These are done over Skype, which is both much more convenient than having to travel to a school and also more personal than trying to help over email or phone.

the magic secret of networking – giving to others

What's your model of networking and how it works? I find that people who don't understand networking and have only attended poorly run events with vapid self-promoters tend to think that networking is fundamentally based on taking. Taking other people's time, taking their business cards and ultimately trying to take their money.

Then there is the set of more seasoned networkers, often very successful business people who are used to the networking of compromise. The tit for tat network. I scratch your back, your scratch mine. You can identify people with this philosophy since they will often counter your offer of help with "as you have helped me, what can I do for you?".

The secret, when you really understand networking, is

that neither of these models are quite right. Many people are surprised to learn that in direct contradiction of those two models, the best networking works on people selflessly giving to others – offering help before someone else does, making a connection for people before they are asked.

You may not be inclined to believe this. You may think that this is wishful thinking on my part, that I just want the world to be this way. In answer, I recommend that you go out and try it. Try thinking of everyone you meet as someone who is helpful and giving and is worth your time to help. Now that I network in this way I find the whole experience to be completely transformed.

By taking the first step and helping others, I find that rarely are people not willing to help me when I in turn need it. By giving indiscriminately I have had amazing opportunities arise for me, facilitated by the people who wouldn't have been top of my list if I had been ordering by those who looked important, or who I thought would be worth keeping sweet so that I could ask them for a favour.

A tangential benefit is that by not feeling the need to judge people as soon as I meet them, and to not have to worry about what they think about me, I can be genuinely myself and make real friendships and connections. And that for me is the real magic secret of networking.

Chopsticks

I often talk at conferences on networking and I love to use this fable, often recited in school assemblies, to illustrate the point.

A man dies and goes to the pearly gates. St. Peter asks him if there's anything he wants before he enters heaven, and the man says he'd like to see hell. So St. Peter takes him down to hell. Hell is a room full of miserable, starving people with a huge banquet table in the middle filled with delicious-looking food. The man asks St. Peter, "Why is THIS hell?" St. Peter replies, "Because the people can only eat the food with 11-foot chopsticks." The man looks around and sees that it's true – everyone is picking up food desperately, but they cannot bring it round and into their mouths. The man then says he's ready to go to heaven, and St. Peter takes him up to a similar room. There is the same huge banquet table in the middle filled with delicious food and the same 11-foot chopsticks. Nothing appears to be different. The man asks St. Peter why this is different from hell, and St. Peter replies, "Here in heaven we all feed each other."

Whatever you think of this as a moral tale, I think it perfectly illustrates how giving makes networking work. You are giving freely, not to get anything in return right now, but to contribute to a system where everyone helps each other and so someone completely unconnected will help you in the future. It's the system of paying it forward.

The other reason that I love to tell that story is that I am surprised by how many people haven't heard it, and who are surprised by the punch line.

Good guys finish last... or do they?

In Adam Grant's brilliant book Give and Take (you can read more about this in the Further Reading section) he talks about a piece of research that was done to find out how successful people were related to how much they gave to others.

One of the first correlations that Grant found confirms the popular maxim that "Good guys finish last". Grant found that the least successful people in the study tended to give more than people placed higher than them in the table. And this makes intuitive sense. We all know people we have worked with, or in our family, who spend so long on other people's problems that they have no time for their own. People who will help a colleague out, so that the colleague's work gets done on time, but their own doesn't. Isn't this how the world works? If you want to be the person who gets to the top of the pile, who worms their way up the greasy pole, don't you need to make sure that you're standing on someone else's head?

Well... no. Because the other correlation that Grant found was that people who featured right at the top of the table also gave more than the people in the middle. So giving seems to have a polarising effect – either you end up last, or, rather more surprisingly, first. So what makes the difference between the givers who impair their own achievements, those who are giving at a cost to themselves and those who are giving and helping themselves in the process?

One thing that clearly makes a difference is having your own agenda to work to. Grant uses the delightful phrase of "enlightened self-interest" to talk about giving in this way. If I am out networking and helping others, it's not going to be very easy for them to help me back unless I have something that I want and I'm open enough about it to let people know what it is.

The key factor though, seems to be how much of their energy people spend helping. It's definitely true that there are some people in this world where if you give an inch, they will take a mile. The key is to not give that mile. The people who found themselves at the bottom of the table were giving all of their energy to others, leaving none for themselves. So what's the alternative? It turns out that there are quite a few ways that you can give to others, without it becoming a drain on your resources. Rather than giving money, or a large amount of time, try to find things that you can do for someone else in 5 minutes or less. I'll give you some examples in the next section.

What can I give?

It's worth having a think about the kind of things that you can give people that don't cost you very much (and sometimes don't cost you anything at all). I tend to give the things that I find most valuable when other people give them to me, namely introductions and book recommendations, but there are many options.

The important thing to remember is where to draw the line. You shouldn't be doing someone's job for them, or trying to make something happen through your exertions rather than theirs. If you give an introduction and they don't follow it up, that's the point to stop and give 5 minutes help to someone else instead. This will help you to keep the right balance between giving, but not giving yourself away.

I personally think that introductions are the top thing that you can give to someone, because there is often no other way to get these (you can't look them up on the internet) and the impact of a timely and well-crafted introduction can be immense. It can be worth thinking through how the person being introduced will feel, and how to best form the introduction so that it produces good results for both parties, but you don't need to run through every possibility and try to make it fool proof. Not every introduction will work out and lead to an amazing opportunity, and that's OK. It won't be because you did something wrong or could have helped someone better. Sometimes things just don't work out. If you only do the foolproof introductions, you will miss some connections that could have by chance worked out brilliantly, and only spared yourself the odd awkward conversation. Trust in the people that you are introducing.

Information is the other most common thing to give that will only take you 5 minutes of time. Unlike physical goods, the magic of information is that it isn't diminished by multiple use – you can give the same fact to hundreds of people and still retain it yourself. Also, despite the advent of Google, which gives us the ability to find anything we care to search for, knowing what to search for still requires the seed of a potent fact. I can search for networking events in London and come across pages of results that I may or may not have time to process. If I know that the best ones are called "Exponential" then my search is cut down considerably. (Shameless plug alert: yes, those are my events.)

Things you can share on networking events will almost always be appreciated, as this is something that you are likely to have in common with anyone you meet. Are there great places that you know about? Do you know someone who runs great events, or has access to event lists or can help along those lines? Is there a great annual event that you just attended but that they could put themselves on the invite list for next year?

Depending on where you are and what areas you overlap in, specialist knowledge might be helpful. Or just interesting knowledge. I was pleasantly surprised when visiting a local coffee shop in Kentish Town to find that the book "The field beneath" after which the coffee shop was named, was available for perusing while you sipped your coffee.

Despite the plethora of online articles (another good recommendation, if you can remember the URL or how to search for it), books still seem to occupy a privileged place in passing on knowledge. If you can recommend someone a good book, you could help them immeasurably. The final chapter in this book contains details of my favourite books on networking, which I recommend to people I meet frequently. Books on sales, management, negotiation and people skills can also be great recommendations.

Sometimes you can help someone by a quick review of something they are doing – a website, and article, a new app. It can take longer than the five minute limit, but I often volunteer to be a beta tester for new services. It helps someone else and I enjoy it, so it's win-win.

Keep the connection

Sometimes you will want an introductory coffee to turn into a longer relationship. Always remember that you can't force this and sometimes it won't work out – trying to stay in touch with someone who doesn't want to be in touch with you never ends well. But if you want to help a relationship along, it's useful to remember that common interests and purpose are what keeps people together. Keith Ferazzi recommends finding a common interest or volunteering to help with a project that they are championing. As someone who runs a lot of volunteer projects, I rarely turn down offers of help!

I'd just finished reading Ferazzi's great book "Never Eat Alone" when I was lucky enough to be introduced to the brilliant technology presenter Maggie Philbin. I was looking for a "mentor" to help with my presenting career and a woman in technology group introduced me to Maggie. When a lot of young people are looking for a "mentor" what they can mean is "someone with a magic answer that can help me achieve all my career goals instantly". That's certainly the stage that I was at. (Incidentally, the best advice I ever got on my presenting career was from Kate Silverton "You're already doing it. What are you worried about?" – I now see this with people time and time again.) Maggie was lovely and helpful and gave me some great tips about using non-traditional formats such as YouTube but it would have been just a single coffee and advice session rather than a connection (that led on to more connections for me) had I not jumped at the chance to help with her fantastic project for introducing young people to technology, Teen Tech. Because I took the opportunity to help her with her agenda, I also found another great event to pass on to companies looking for ways to give back, or people looking to get involved with promoting technology.

unusual ideas for gaining confidence

I wasn't sure whether to include this chapter or not, but decided that I would on the grounds that inspiration can come from anywhere. Feel free to skip it if you're just after straight-forward how-to networking tips.

The key to becoming good at networking, discovering the benefits and hence being driven to keep going is to simply start. Once you have found your way, you will find looking back at your initial fears an interesting exercise. ("I thought what??"). Until then, all kinds of experiences and training can help you to gain confidence and try new things.

Here are a few of the things that have helped me become more rounded as a person and more willing to engage with others. Many of them focus on taking attention and focus away from logic and reason, and living more "in the body" allowing you to be more spontaneous. None are spiritual or religious, but many need to be dived into with a sense of faith in not knowing what will happen.

Exercise

Ever since I was at university, exercise has been recommended as a great way of getting out of yourself, and of gaining perspective on life. It was a shame for me then that I had decided that it was not something that I did, or that would be possible for me. My particular bête-noir was jogging. I could logically admit that I was no less physically capable of it than others, but I held myself mentally incapable. I just didn't have the patience, stamina, whatever.

Experimenting with meditation (see below) allowed me to become curious about my resistance to running, and curious to whether I could in fact ignore the fact that it hurt, rather than trying to overcome it. I've just this week run for 30 minutes every other day, and it allows me to start on a high – something productive done before breakfast.

Lots of other forms of exercise can provoke the same reaction: swimming, aerobics, yoga. Julia Cameron (author of The Artist's Way, a fabulous book for creative people) recommends walking for twenty minutes at least once a week, to clear your head and get new perspective.

Yoga

Yoga and meditation have also long been on my list of "things that I don't do". Like almost everyone, I have focussed on the things that came easily at the expense of those that I found difficult. Flexibility was a key one of those. I changed my mind and became determined to try yoga after success at running – maybe I was also missing something here. Luckily I was offered a free class from Luci Beatty at http://relaxrestore.info/ via the amazing social sharing site Streetbank.

The reason that I mention yoga is that I think that a lot of issues with confidence in social situations come from over-thinking at the expense of just living in your body. As well as being really healthy (you can find pages and pages listing the benefits if you search on the internet), yoga helps you to connect with yourself and become calmer.

Meditation

Meditation seems to be at the centre of a renaissance. Having long been considered something for hippies seeking spiritual enlightenment, we are just starting to uncover lots of scientific research on the benefits of meditation as a practice, removed from any religious connections. Coupling this with the onset of mobile phone apps that allow you to meditate anywhere (even on the tube during your commute) and suddenly loads more people are becoming converts.

I started using the Headspace meditation app about 6 months ago. Like when I had previously tried meditation, I didn't really get it to start with, which is really normal. I had a go every so often, and sometimes felt that my head was a bit clearer. Once I had started thinking of meditation as something that could be useful to me, I started to see more people using it. A local coding academy ran meditation every morning. One of my senior colleagues told me that he used a quick three minute breathing exercise to combat project management stress.

I learnt by reading more about meditation that curiosity is key to unlocking it. When we aim directly at a goal and don't get there, we quickly give up. If we can instead be opening to seeing what happens, something new might emerge in that space.

I don't know exactly when or how the transition happened but I now use the Headspace app every day and have had some great experiences with becoming more accepting and more creative. I am also now entertained rather than annoyed by the somewhat zen-like nature of it, that you can get the benefits only by letting go of your need for an objective outcome.

By opening my mind to more options, I have also really helped myself to be able to communicate with a wider range of people – it is hard to form a bond with someone if you are too busy thinking that the interests that they have are unscientific nonsense.

Public speaking training

Public speaking is similar to networking, and not so similar. I know people who excel with a group of people in a room, but quake at taking the stage. Similarly I have friends and colleagues who can almost hide themselves behind a "performance" on stage, but feel exposed when simply having a chat with others.

The common root of people's issues with both of these activities is confidence. This means that working on overcoming your fear of public speaking could well help you with networking. How less scary will it seem to have a conversation with someone after you've been brave enough to give a talk from the stage?

Lots of tips that you will learn for public speaking will cross over into networking. I have also given talks to novice speakers and some tips jump out immediately as being identical for both – practice, projecting confidence (eye contact etc.) and speaking clearly, for example. If possible, find a club for speakers who are starting out and practising – Speaking Out (speakingoutevents.com) in London is a great example. By meeting up with other people who are learning and at a similar stage to you, you will feel much more supported, and hopefully that will spill over into your networking too.

Acting training

I don't think acting training is something that most people would consider. I certainly haven't tried it in order to improve my networking, although there's definitely a link in my case between having become better at networking and having the confidence to try things like this.

There is a new trend of acting schools and teachers offering to teach in business. You may have seen the adverts for training in business speaking at the Royal Academy of Dramatic Art. My acting tutor also teaches politicians.

Learning more about acting has surprised me, as it's not the skill that I thought it was. Acting is much more about understanding people and how they interact with each other than it is about learning lines, or being able to project your voice or fake an emotion. It is for this reason that I found several ideas useful for networking within the course.

1. "Nerves are vanity". This beautiful phrase explains succinctly that if you are nervous it is because you are worrying too much about yourself, and your own performance. Try thinking instead about the person who you are talking to.

2. When characters are engaging in a scene, they often want something from the other person – they certainly want an outcome for themselves in general. They are not trying to convey a point to the audience. I've found this a really enlightening thought and look at other people through new eyes, trying to ascertain their motives, trying to learn what they want to achieve. It's almost definitely not the same as what I am wanting to do.

3. Lots of acting instruction talks about status. This is a very interesting idea. Thinking about it in this way, you can see interactions between people as status transactions. When we interact with people we are always trying to ascertain our own status and behave in the appropriate way. We each choose a status to act as a defence – high status people are trying to send the message "don't bite me, or else" and low status people "don't bite me, I'm not worth it". By studying this, we can learn to modify our behaviour and get on with people better. If we are accidentally coming across as stand-offish, we can choose to

lower our status and be more welcoming. If we are nervous of other people we can use high status behaviours, such as maintaining eye contact, to make us feel more secure.

All acting training is well known for taking people out of their comfort zone. CityLit in London run brilliant courses, open to people of all levels. I have met accountants, receptionists and people from all walks of life who are interested in trying something new. Why not try it? You might like it, and if you don't, at least just chatting to a room full of people will seem less scary.

See something inspirational

I read an awful lot of business and self-improvement books. I get at least several useful tips from each of these, but I also get something else. I get motivation to carry on with what I'm planning. I find that reading books by other people who have achieved what they set out to do, against the personal challenges that afflicted them, reassures me that perhaps I should keep going for a bit longer and see what happens.

As people we can find inspiration all over the place. A sunset, a view from a mountain, animals and plants. I think it's important to not disregard this ("I should be doing some work!") but instead to draw inspiration from it.

All forms of art affect people similarly, whether it is pictures, music or film and performing arts. Why not try to combine your networking with a cultural pursuit?

If you are networking at conferences or other events with speakers, you are likely to find some of their stories inspiring. Accomplished and especially professional speakers have put a lot of work into distilling the essence of what they have learnt just so that they can communicate a message to you. Let it inspire you!

A favourite form of inspiration for many people I know is watching the TED talks on YouTube. TED is a conference in California that was started with a specific set of rules for the speakers. Talks must not exceed 18 minutes in length, speakers should not be elevated above the other participants and there would be no Q&A sessions with the speakers, instead participants would discuss the topics and themes with each other. This format has led to many amazing talks by a wide range of people: business owners, athletes, authors and many more. Why not take a look and be inspired by what humans can achieve?

Try something new

It was at a local TED event, TEDxRussellSquare, that I came across a concept that was so straightforward I simply couldn't believe that I hadn't realised it before. If you want to be a different person i.e. if you want to change and develop, you need to do things differently. This statement is self-evidently true, and I found it revelationary. Why is someone else different to you? Because they behave in a different way. So how do you become different? By doing things differently. That's not to say that it will be easy to do things differently, or I suppose in some cases even possible, but it's nice to understand that the process is that simple.

So why not try something undirected and new? You might learn something about yourself, and at the least you can use it as a topic of conversation ("I read this crazy book on networking and as a result I…"). If you wish you were more arty, do something arty. If you pine for the outdoors, try cycling or hillwalking. It's incredible how powerful it can be just to disrupt the patterns that you have formed that define who you are. Be someone different for a bit, just to see what happens.

going one step further

As I grew to love networking more and more, and started to see what amazing benefits you could get from it, I moved from being a consumer of networking events to a creator of them. In 2012 I started my own networking company, Tech Talkfest, to help connect the thriving start-up scene in London. I hunted out speakers, enjoying the opportunity it gave me to set agendas that were interesting to me and the chance I had to give a platform to people doing really interesting things in the start-up space.

I worried terribly at my first event that no-one would come, and I would have to phone my friends up just to prevent the room from looking empty. I needn't have worried. With some basic marketing from me, and some unsolicited help from the event platform I chose (Eventbrite, who have been lovely to me ever since), over 130 people signed up for a new event run by an unknown person. What a great way to learn that everyone needs networking events, and that you can help a whole room full of people at once by setting one up.

By running my own events, I learned something else that I had been told, but hadn't seen in action. Being the person running the event makes your own networking even more powerful. As the host it is incumbent on you to make sure all of your guests are having a great time, which means running round to meet and chat with as many of them as possible. You also have a brilliant reason to connect with them outside of the event, and you have easy access to their contact details because you're the organiser.

None of the ideas that I suggest in this chapter are essential for being a good, or even a great networker. But if you feel ready to take it to the next level, you'll find they are very simple to implement and can help to enhance the benefits of what you have already learned.

Now that my events are becoming more well-known and I have taken some other steps to raise my profile, I have people coming along to my events in order to meet me. Fabulous! It feels almost as if as you get better at networking, it starts to come to you rather than you having to chase it.

Create your own events

I first heard about the concept of creating your own events in the bible of networking, Never Eat Alone by Keith Ferazzi. For him, it was an obvious step to move to being at the centre of a network. Sometimes you will also find that whereas at other events you can end up hiding round the edges despite your best intentions, at your own event you are likely to feel spurred on to make sure it is a success. You will be immediately flipped into the "thinking about others" role that works so well for making connections.

Does the thought of being in charge of an event scare you rigid? Well here's why it shouldn't. If you are running the event, you are in charge of it. You can decide how many people attend, what they will do and what the atmosphere will be like. If you are in charge, you set the tone. Having attended many events that I found unwelcoming and cold, I now relish the opportunity to make sure that people feel welcomed at events that I run. I look for people who seem to be struggling (or perhaps just temporarily on their own) and make connections for them. I smile at people.

I sometimes run events with hundreds of people in a room, but that might not be for everyone. If you find large events impersonal, why not set up an intimate dinner or an informal social group? Here are some options.

A subgroup at a conference

Have you ever heard about the best networking at a conference being done outside of the official events? Have you felt jealous when everyone seems to be attending some invite only dinner reception afterwards? I know I have.

What I have learned is that these are simply events set up by someone who wants to build a network, or have some fun, or most often both. Now that you know that, what's to prevent the person organising the after-conference party being you? That way you will always be invited.

A conference has put a lot of the basics in place to allow you to group people together, making it much easier than organising an event cold. Most of the relevant people in the industry will be there, and lots of them will be looking for things to do in the evening, especially if they have flown in from overseas and need to stay over. There may be a messaging service that you can use to tell people about your sub-event, or you could even print up some cards and hand them out to people that you meet.

It never hurts to try out organising something like this. If lots of people attend, fabulous. If not many attend then you can't have damaged your reputation by very much because no-one was there to see it! And small groups can be more intimate and set you up for better networking.

Once you've organised a few things and got the hang of it, why not get in touch with the official conference organiser and offer your services? They are likely to be delighted to have something else to offer to their attendees, and if you become part of the official program you may get listed in the brochure or announced over the tannoy – if you want more people to attend that is. If you liked it exclusive, you can keep it that way.

A social or dinner meetup

If there's one thing that I hope I have managed to convey in this book, it's that whenever a group of people are gathered together and meeting each other – it is networking. You don't need a formal event with a fancy title to make it so.

So if you are organising an event, why not make it one that you like? Organise an event around a hobby or a table of people over dinner. Or both!

This is such an important area that there are even a couple of startups working in this space who can help you to facilitate your dinner. 9others has a format for a ten person dinner (yourself and 9 others, geddit!) that started in the startup and investment space and is now expanding into other industries.

Tablecrowd is an online platform that allows you to set a theme, a location and a price and then people from their network (and yours!) can sign up to come along. Dinners are always a popular way to network in a more social way.

There is another new website that is really useful for organising informal social events – meetup.com. This allows you to set a date, time and place and then people can sign up to come to your meetup. You can't charge for tickets, but this is a great site for collecting people together around a common passion. Once you have an account people who are interested in your meetings but who can't make the ones currently listed can sign up to "follow" you and hear about any new events you post.

I personally really recommend this way of starting out. Networking is always best when it is fun, and socialising over dinner is a great way to make it so. Keith Ferazzi, as you may have guessed from the title of his book ("Never Eat Alone") was very keen on networking over meals. He would invite people over to his house every evening and make the event a mix of old friends, new acquaintances and everything in between. Rather than people feeling awkward at having been mixed in with new people, everyone found it refreshing and often made really useful contacts that they then carried forward with them.

An online group

Lots of people can find it tricky to meet in real life when they are balancing lots of commitments. It's easy to see how the young, single go-getters can be up and out at a breakfast event and then stay out late drinking or having dinner but as you get older and have commitments this can become much more tricky.

A great solution that takes advantage of technology is to set up an online group. As with a live event, you can start this yourself quite simply. The technology is free and easy to use (I would recommend groups.google. com) – all you need to do is to create a group and get people to sign up!

I have found with new groups that people are often quite shy to contribute early on, so you will need quite a few people to get a good discussion going (maybe about ten times the number you would have at an event) and to start with at least you may need to seed conversations to solicit people's opinions and get them talking.

Once you get to know people online you may well find that they are keen to meet up in real life too. This can make a great hybrid space. As people get to know each other better in each sphere, it reinforces their relationship in the other one i.e. chatting online helps people feel more relaxing when meeting up for coffee, and meeting for coffee means that they know each other better and can have more trusting conversations online.

A registry or other service

The great resource that you can share with other people through networking is information. As I'm sure you've found when you searched for something online, one of the problems with information is that it goes out of date quickly and relevant, up-to-date information can be hard to find.

Putting together useful resources for people can be a real help, and if you give them a way to contact people you might get some interesting contacts from this too. Or you might want to have a notice-board or similar as part of your registry where people can post comments and connect with each other.

As with finding a theme for an event, you might not think

immediately that you have any specialisms to create a
registry around. Well why not document all the useful
things that you are finding on your journey into learning
about networking? Business help and resources are
something that almost everyone has in common and
if you can build a useful site and update the content
regularly people will start to find you through the search
engines.

Training / helping other people with networking

Another type of event that I think you can usefully set
up is a training session. You may feel that you are not
ready to start training on networking, having only just
read a book, but this is not the case at all. People often
mistakenly feel that only "experts" can pass on useful
knowledge, but the more experience you get in an
area, the more that you realise that the concept of an
"expert" can often be very misleading, and just because
someone knows something in great detail does not
mean that they are a good teacher for new starters.

If you are just one step ahead of people who are starting
out, that is a great place to teach them from. You can
share your personal experiences and develop rapport by
having only very recently left the same boat as them. In

terms of what to teach, you need only a few key points to make a good training session. Why not pick three or so networking tips that have really helped for you, and develop a session including your personal stories and a chance for people to try them out? After I had read Never Eat Alone, I did exactly this – running a session at City Business Library giving people examples of pitches and introductory questions with gaps left for them to use these ideas to introduce themselves to everyone else in the room.

Raise your profile

I have mentioned earlier in the book about how you can often make better connections at a conference or other event with speakers by ignoring the rush for the stage and instead networking with other attendees.

There is another way that you can take advantage of the tendency for everyone in the room to want to talk with the speakers and that's to become one! Like everything else in this book this is entirely optional and given that you main aim is to learn how to have fun while networking, it will only be helpful for you to do this if you are going to enjoy it. You are much better off attending an event as a guest and chatting to people quietly and happily than being miserable on and off stage.

Speaking is of course just one way of raising your profile, but most ways require you to take a leap of faith in yourself. There is no-one currently in the public eye who has not at some point thought "Why would anyone listen to me? What do I have to say that is different?". You will find out what it is that you can share with others by trying it out and putting yourself forwards.

The key to raising your profile is to make contact with large numbers of people, which is why speaking at events (or, even better, on TV) is so good for it. It's not the only way though. By contributing to groups and discussions online people will get to hear your views, and if you prefer one to one networking, you can build a large network this way – it will take longer, but it will be more powerful for it.

next steps

So now you know a whole load more about networking, what are you going to do with it? In this final chapter I've put together some simple ideas for next steps that you can take to start yourself on your networking adventure. (Remember: it's going to be fun!)

I recommend starting with the idea in the list that most appeals to you and gradually working your way through them as you gain confidence. I do recommend trying out all the different ways of networking – at an event, making connections with people directly and setting up your own events. As you network more and more you will start to get a feel for which way works best for you; you will develop your own style.

Find out who you are

Put aside thirty minutes, either at the office or when you have some time at home, to sit down and think about who you are and what you enjoy.

Make a word cloud (**http://www.zoefcunningham. com/blog/word-cloud**) to list out what you enjoy, and start to put together the pieces of your life into a short straightforward introduction.

For the purpose of networking it's good to have an introduction that is under sixty seconds long (or even shorter if you can!). Work out the key things about yourself that you need to communicate (What services do you offer? What are you good at? What do you enjoy?) and practice putting them into a concise introduction. Why not try this out on people when you meet them?

Register for an event

Learning how to networking at events is a great skill. Pick an event that you are already attending, or book into a new one, and designate it your "training" event. Go along and try out some ideas from this book – see what happens with your pitch, try some introductory questions and maybe even try leaving a conversation to talk with someone else.

As this is a training event, aim for the event that you can find that you think will be the most fun. Not the most useful, most relevant or with the best contacts, the most fun. You will help yourself more by going to an event and learning how to have fun than by trying to make the most or best contacts.

Obviously I recommend Exponential's events if you are based in London, but have a look on Google too or ask people for recommendations.

Reach out to ten people

There are two basic ways to meet people: in person at events, where you can meet people by change and directly, when you can have more control over who you meet. Think about what you want to achieve and think of some people or organisations that can help you. Try also to think of people you have come across who may be fun to meet – perhaps speakers you have seen who you really connected with. If you are looking for inspiration you could also look at connections of your connections on LinkedIn – does anyone you know, know someone who looks interesting?

Make a list of maybe ten people you would like to meet. Try to be creative about who can help you. You will have more success if you try to reach out to people who are approached less often than others. Then reach out to them to see whether you can make a connection. You can often find out people's email addresses by using a common company format, or if they have a connection in common with you may be able to get an email intro or their phone number. Sometimes you can get hold of people by phone by calling their main office switchboard (although often you will be met by someone screening for cold calls in that case).

You might want to get in touch via a website. Twitter is great for informal contacts – some people respond more quickly to contacts there, although some may not see it. I personally find LinkedIn an amazing way to contact new people. They can see your entire profile and so find out what you are about, and also you can send a customised message (although limited in length) directly to them.

Reach out internally

Unless you work for yourself or for a very small company, chances are that there are plenty of people that you work with that you have never spoken to. If you work for a very large organisation then there are probably people that you are in awe of and feel out of reach to you (for example the senior executive).

There is no end to the help that you might be able to get by reaching out internally. Make a list of five or so people who could be useful to you as a collaborator, sponsor or mentor, or who you just think might be cool to meet and see if they have time for a coffee.

All networking books are full of stories of people being surprised by how accessible even the CEO is, if you just ask, and about how they are often inspired by enthusiastic employees who want to know how they can contribute more to the company. As CEO of a company I have to re-iterate just how true this is! I go one step further and try to make it clear to people that there is time free in my calendar for people to come and see me whenever suits them – and I still get people saying "I know you are probably too busy but…". Obviously in a larger organisation it won't necessarily be possible for the CEO to issue an open invitation like this, but the same sentiment will be there and they will really appreciate contact from people within the organisation who are trying to make links.

Reconnect

Even without trying to "network" we all make hundreds of new contacts all the time. The difference is that most of us let these connections lapse, even with people that we got on really well with. As you now know, networking is not all about meeting new people or trying to have coffee with the CEO – it's about forming real and lasting relationships with people.

So pick up again with an old friend or colleague – reconnect and find out what they are up to. People lives are constantly changing… you may find all kinds of new links between you that you hadn't previously realised.

Get online

In just a five to ten minute session you can start to make an impact on your online profile.

If you are new to networking and connecting online I would really recommend that your first port of call is LinkedIn. Registering and setting up your basic information (including a photograph!) should take no more than five minutes. By linking in to your contacts you will be automatically engaging in light touch networking. I've often been pleasantly surprised to be reminded of someone I haven't seen for a while when they connect on LinkedIn. You can fill in a more detailed profile later on – why not do it five minutes at a time?

If you're already happily dabbling in online connections, why not start putting together a social media plan? That doesn't need to be scary or time consuming. Pick a couple of platforms to concentrate on and work out how you can put out regular updates and connect with people. Can you schedule a regular time each day (or one or twice a week?) to give a brief update? Or would you prefer to use a service like Hootsuite, where you can set up in advance some updates to go out over the next few months?

Make the network yourself

Being the event organiser really is a brilliant way to connect with people (and give something back!). Why not start planning an event that you can run? You can start small by finding a great restaurant to host a dinner gathering, or a bar or café where you could have some drinks. Think through your contacts to see if anyone has something that they would be happy to share. Don't worry that asking them is an imposition – I have not yet come across someone who isn't massively flattered to be asked to speak. One of the things I love most about running events and writing and filming interviews is the ability to showcase all my very talented friends.

Over the next year, why not try a few event formats? Any that work really well you can run as a series and start to build up a community.

further reading

In my networking journey, I have been encouraged and inspired by the great number of great networking books that have been written. Books are not only a great way to get more tips, or new takes on ones you already know, but also a fabulous way to keep up your motivation to stick with networking even when you find it difficult.

Here is a brief summary of some of my favourite networking books:

Never Eat Alone, Keith Ferazzi

Never Eat Alone is the absolute bible of networking. I came across this book in an introductory talk on networking by a lady who has been voted the most connected woman in Britain.

I have never met anyone who is as assiduous a networker as Keith Ferazzi. From when he gets up – early, so he call across to contacts in different time zones – to when he ends the day – with a cross-contact networking dinner, mixing up old friends and new acquaintances – he is a non-stop whirlwind of networking.

What I find most inspiring about this book is that you can do a tenth (or even less!) of the amount of networking that Keith does and still be amazing.

Give and Take, Adam Grant

Described as "the rising star of positive psychology", Adam Grant is a professor at the Wharton School of the University of Pennsylvania. His book talks about how to be successful through helping other people, and that this is best way to help yourself.

I recommend this book if you are at unsure of the assertion that this is the magic secret of networking!

To Sell is Human, Dan Pink

My first foray into networking came about because I changed into a sales role. This was a big move for me, and I learnt that a lot of the views that I'd previously held on sales were completely outdated and in some cases just incorrect.

In this lovely book for non-salespeople, Dan Pink explains how sales is a natural activity that we all engage in, whether it's closing a multi-million pound deal or just trying to persuade someone of our business idea.

The Go Giver

The Go-Giver is a short sweet book, which outlines the five principles of "go giving" in the form of a story. A quick and entertaining read if you have a small gap in your schedule.

The Tipping Point: How Little Things Can Make a Big Difference, Malcolm Gladwell

One of the books that launched Malcolm Gladwell's career, *The Tipping Point* explains how networks between us allow ideas to spread. It explains the principles behind this, including ideas such as the value of people who form links between different groups and social circles. This isn't a "how to" book on networking but it has some interesting ideas and is worth a read.

How to Win Friends and Influence People, Dale Carnegie

I find it hard to believe that *How to Win Friends and Influence People* was written in 1936. The world was different in many ways, but people, it turns out, were exactly the same. When I first read this book many years ago I was amazed by how often we can get dealing with people wrong without realising it.

This is a great book about people, and networking is all about people. A classic.

Zoe Cunningham has 15 years' experience working in the technology sector and is currently Managing Director of Softwire Technology. In 2013 she was named as one of the 100 most influential people in Tech City, selected by the BBC as the Brightest Woman in Britain and she accompanied Prime Minister David Cameron on his trade delegation to China.

Zoe is a passionate advocate of networking and in 2012 founded Tech Talkfest to connect influential people in the technology world. She now runs the private members' network Exponential.

Zoe Cunningham has trained as an actor at RADA, The Actors Centre and City Lit. She acted in her first one woman show at the Tristan Bates Theatre in February 2015 to critical acclaim and subsequently toured the show to Brighton Fringe. Other theatre credits include Mrs Arbuthnot in Oscar Wilde's *A Woman of No Importance* and social worker Moira in Chris Lee's modern work *Shallow Slumber*. On film she has appeared opposite Steve Coogan and Anna Friel in Michael Winterbottom's *The Look of Love*, and has played Clara, a confidence trickster, in indie Brit-flick *Carbon Foxes*.

Zoe is a regular contributor to several technology blogs and has had articles published online at the *Guardian*, *Computer Weekly* and *The Huffington Post*. She has presented tech radio shows for Age UK's *The Wireless*, Zone One Radio and Shoreditch Radio and has been a guest presenter on *BBC Click*.

"Want to impress your customers, your colleagues, and your boss with your clear, straight-to-the-point, dazzling writing? Then smack yourself into action with this book, a must for all business writers in the digital age."

Barry Dwyer, Senior Lecturer in Management, London Metropolitan University Business School

Pbk, £7.99, ISBN 9781910692455

Bestselling author **Andreas Loizou** delivers the first in
a groundbreaking new series of concise, forthright and
wholly practical titles that give you the real skills you
need to succeed in business. Business writing is often
terrifying. Many of us get blocked, lost, anxious and
confused when forced to put our thoughts into words.
In our frantic, numbers-driven world, the importance of
clear writing is often over-looked. Here are the tools and
techniques to improve the quality and speed of your
writing. Whether it's a two-line email or a two-hundred

page report, your communication skills will rocket and you'll have the toolbox you require to pitch effectively whatever your business. Learn how to attract readers and, once they're completely in your thrall, turn them into loyal followers. Your confidence will grow as you learn how to structure and plan your writing. You'll get clear messages across quickly. And you'll do it with style.